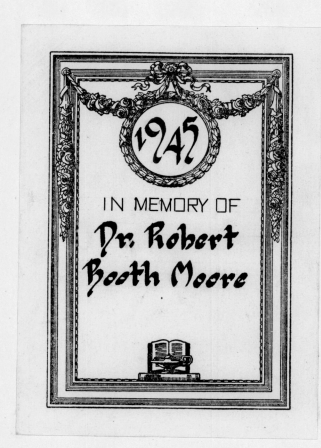

MEN
WITHOUT GUNS

THE MAN WITHOUT A GUN—Lawrence Beall Smith.

MEN
WITHOUT GUNS

Text by

DeWITT MACKENZIE

War Analyst of The Associated Press

Descriptive Captions by

Major CLARENCE WORDEN

Medical Department of the United States Army

Foreword by

Major General NORMAN T. KIRK

Surgeon General of the United States Army

ILLUSTRATED WITH 137 PLATES FROM THE ABBOTT
COLLECTION OF PAINTINGS OWNED BY THE UNITED
STATES GOVERNMENT

Philadelphia THE BLAKISTON COMPANY Toronto
1945

Contents

Illustrations

Foreword

By Major General NORMAN T. KIRK, M.C., U.S.A.
The Surgeon General

No ARTIST ever had a more worthy subject for his brush than did the twelve distinguished painters whose canvases on Army Medicine are reproduced in this volume.

Unequivocally and without fear of contradiction, I say with pride and reverence that one of the greatest contributions to victory has been made by the doctors, nurses and enlisted men of the Army Medical Department. Without their tireless devotion to duty, their courage and complete disregard for self-safety, the Medical Department would not be able to point today to a record of achievement unmatched in the long history of warfare.

Because of the heroism and skill of the men and women portrayed between the covers of this book, countless thousands of our fighting men have survived wounds that would have meant certain death in the last war. Their deeds on the battlefields, in front-line medical units and in the great general hospitals have done much to frustrate and discourage a murderous enemy intent upon destroying us with every diabolically ingenious instrument of war he could devise.

This volume is titled "*Men Without Guns.*" It is a fitting name for a book that tells the story of men and women who fight with surgical instruments and drugs — penicillin, sulfa, plasma, atabrine and other life-saving medical agents.

The twelve distinguished artists who have produced this Abbott Collection of Paintings of Army Medicine have told the story faithfully. Their paintings constitute an authentic and valuable contemporary history of Army Medicine in the war and a priceless archival treasure.

Some day, in all probability, the original paintings will hang proudly in our nation's capital for all to see. Meanwhile, it is most gratifying to me and my associates in the Medical Department that these paintings are here reproduced so that so many of us can always have them with us in our homes.

This collection is an eloquent testimonial to the enterprise and foresight of Lieutenant Colonel Howard F. Baer, M.A.C., who conceived it, to Abbott Laboratories, who sponsored it, to the War Department, which encouraged it, to Associated American Artists whose director, Mr. Reeves Lewenthal, supervised it and to Charles Downs of Abbott Laboratories who has so ably brought it to the attention of the public. To Mr. S. DeWitt Clough, President of Abbott, the Medical Department and the Surgeon General, personally, are very grateful.

The Surgeon General and His Staff

Seated, left to right

Brig. Gen. Raymond W. Bliss, M.C.

Col. James R. Hudnall, M.C.

Brig. Gen. Fred W. Rankin, M.C.

Brig. Gen. Edward Reynolds, M.A.C.

Brig. Gen. Raymond A. Kelser, V.C.

Maj. Gen. Norman T. Kirk, M.C.

Maj. Gen. George F. Lull, M.C.

Standing, left to right

Brig. Gen. Charles C. Hillman, M.C.

Brig. Gen. Hugh J. Morgan, M.C.

Col. Robert J. Carpenter, M.C.

Maj. Gen. Robert H. Mills, D.C.

Brig. Gen. James S. Simmons, M.C.

1

Introducing the Corpsman

IT TAKES vast courage for a fighting-man to go into action.

He must have a stout heart who leaps from his fox-hole with the bloody dawn of an offensive and pushes forward in a storm of bullets, shells and bombs until he comes to close grips with the enemy; or who races up from the sea through the minefield of a landing-beach under a hurricane of fire; or who stands by his post as his ship, with guns flaming, drives her nose right into the crimsoning waters of a beach-head; or yet who flies into action across a flak-filled sky.

All this demands surpassing heroism. But a very special fortitude is needed by the man who goes into battle as a non-combatant.

The tension of the man-at-arms is eased by the very fact that his brain is juggling with the life-or-death problems of offense and defense, and because his hands are occupied with the use of his weapons. Fear gives way to the hot spirit of strife.

It's a wholly different proposition for the non-combatant, however. He is beset by all the anxiety of the soldier—more, for that matter, because he likely hasn't even a club with which to defend himself—and lacks the relief which comes from having his mind engaged with battle.

These unarmed forces—trained to defend themselves with their bare hands in emergency—form a vital part of Uncle Sam's mighty fighting-machine. They are the paradox of war, for their mission is to save human life, and not to take it. This labor of devotion they perform with few headlines, though their deeds are epic.

It is largely with these unsung heroes that this story deals, and so without further preliminary I give you the United States Army Medical Department—*Men Without Guns*.

Of course this great non-combatant organization comprises many different elements, just as does the army. There are the men who actually go into battle with the troops and rush to the thick of the fray at the call of help from the wounded. There are the corpsmen who in an emergency may operate on an injured man in a fox-hole under heavy fire. There are the surgeons and doctors who labor to the point of utter exhaustion about the operating tables of stations which are under bombing and shell-fire in the forward areas. There are nurses who work in

constant danger of death. And then there are others who risk their lives no less certainly in fighting the terrible diseases which plague the steaming, stinking jungles and other primeval sections of our globe.

Those are the sensational aspects of the work—the big thrills—but that's not the whole of it by a long way. Just as the soldier on the firing line is backed by the organization of the home-front, so does the corpsman in action have behind him the vast Army Medical Department over which presides Surgeon General Norman T. Kirk in Washington. The thousand and one ramifications of this wonderfully synchronized medical machine are what make possible the corpsman's activities in the theatres of war.

So this is neither solely a tale of heroic deeds—though they figure largely in the saving of life—nor is it a history of the Army Medical Department. Rather it is an impressionistic report, done in pictures and in words, of the magnificent service rendered by the Department as a whole in the second World War. Its primary object is to give to the folk at home an account of how the health of their boys in the far-away zones of conflict is safeguarded, and of how those soldiers who have been hurt are cared for.

Now it isn't the purpose either of the artists or the writer to handle this story with gloves. There will be many harsh things to see and read, for that is war. It's no use for us to sit back home here in comfort and security and not know the truth about what our lads encounter.

There has been a disposition in some quarters to shield the public from disturbing facts, but this book has nothing to conceal. We take our lead from Major General Kirk himself, for he has said:

"The American public should be told the truth about what war does to fighting men. It should know that some of our men are struck down by disease, that they lose arms or legs and that they come home nervous invalids.

"The public should also know that in no war have soldiers been given more scientific, painstaking medical care and more human understanding. They will continue to get that care and understanding wherever they are."

So, while the good news will far outweigh the bad in this chronicle, you will be told the truth as we know it. Some of it is mighty tough to contemplate. For example, here's an incident which was given me by Major General George F. Lull, Deputy Surgeon General of the Army Medical Department, while we were chatting in his Washington office. The conversation had turned toward the courage of the corpsman and his ingenuity in meeting unusual emergencies, and I asked the General for a story to illustrate these points. He looked at me speculatively for a moment and then said in his direct manner of speech:

"All right, I'll tell you a story. And it's one we investigated and confirmed."

He then related the experience of a battalion surgeon in the Southwest Pacific. The Japanese had swarmed down from strong points on a hill and surrounded the battalion. One of our soldiers had an arm so badly torn that amputation was necessary. Here indeed was a case to test the nerve and inventiveness of the surgeon, for not only was he without instruments but the whole area in which they were surrounded was being swept by enemy fire.

However, the doctor got his men into a fox-hole, and then hunted about for some sort of instrument. The only thing he could find was an ax, but that didn't stop him, for a life was at stake. He sterilized the ax with hot alcohol, gave the wounded soldier ether—and then removed the arm while bullets and pieces of shell screamed over his fox-hole operating room.

Three days later the battalion was relieved, and the soldier's life was saved!

Then there was a somewhat similar case which was carried by the press out of Bougainville, in the Solomon Islands. This concerned a medical corps major who amputated both legs of a wounded man with a hunting knife under fire. I'm not going to name the major here, for it hardly seems fair to the thousands of other Medical Corps officers who have performed equally heroic tasks. But let the sergeant who had a hand in the case tell about it in a soldier's blunt way:

"He (the Major) removed the left leg below the knee and the right at the knee. It took two hours. I gave plasma to that boy, who was conscious all the time. He was awfully brave. He screamed just a little when the Major cut, because he was in great pain. But he took it very well. He was an ammunition carrier hit by a mortar."

However, these are merely by way of passing illustration. We are getting ahead of our story a bit, and we shall be dealing with plenty of the crudities of war in subsequent chapters. So let's return to our muttons, as the Englishman says.

The idea of recording the work of the Army Medical Department in art really had its genesis when Lt. Colonel Howard F. Baer, of the Medical Administrative Corps, saw the new moon over his left shoulder and made a mighty wish which came true. The way of it was this:

One of Colonel Baer's great friends is another Howard Baer, the widely known artist. They aren't relatives but the likeness of names is just a peculiar coincidence which brought them together in the first place. Well, back in May of '43 Colonel Baer discovered Artist Baer busy doing some paintings for a collection of naval aviation art which was being created for the United States Navy as a gift by the Abbott Laboratories, a large pharmaceutical supply house in Chicago.

Right there was where Colonel Baer made his big wish. It was that the Army Medical Department might be blessed with a similar project. One of his main reasons was that at this time a great deal of publicity was being given to general war work, and people were being urged to get out of non-essential industries and take war jobs.

Naturally that didn't help employment in the plants which were making medical supplies. In fact it hurt, because it was difficult to prevent workers who were making hypodermic needles, surgical instruments, surgical dressings, atabrine, and the hundred and one other things urgently needed by the Medical Department, from believing that much greater service could be rendered by leaving these jobs and taking others in plants manufacturing bombs and like instruments of war.

Baer, the Colonel, talked the idea over with Baer, the Artist, and the latter brought a third party into the discussions—Reeves Lewenthal, president of the Associated American Artists, who had much to do with the Abbott program for the Navy. The Colonel raised with Lewenthal the question of whether it would be possible to get someone to sponsor an Army Medical Department project, and the upshot was that Abbott offered to back this further undertaking—a very costly affair, by the way. The approval of Surgeon General Kirk was secured and there was begun the great work which you see recorded in part in the pictures reproduced in this book.

The plan was the most ambitious of its kind ever carried out, for it covered not only Medical Department activities of the home-front but reached into the fighting theatres of Europe, the Pacific, India, Burma and China. Among the subjects dealt with were the training of physicians and enlisted men in the schools at Carlisle Barracks, Pennsylvania, and Camp Barkeley, Texas, among others; the production of those all-important medical and surgical supplies; the movement of men and supplies in combat theatres; the general hospitals, including operative surgery, convalescence, and rehabilitation and occupational therapy; the hospital ship; the army nurse; aviation medicine; and, of course, the gripping story of how the Medical Corps performed its mission of mercy amidst the hell of the actual battle zones.

Twelve American artists were selected to carry out this program, and in 1944 they produced a large number of striking paintings and sketches out of which was built the collection that Abbott Laboratories presented to the government. S. DeWitt Clough, president of Abbott's and himself a patron of the arts, described the gift as "a tribute to the tremendous accomplishment of the Army Medical Department in saving the lives of scores of thousands of American soldiers who would be dead today but for the vast improvement of medical service in this over any previous war."

It is a remarkable thing that none of the artists who went to the fighting fronts was killed or injured, for all of them saw action. All were in the midst of gunfire. Robert Benney, for instance, was in the thick of the battle of Saipan. It's even more remarkable that none of them suffered grave illness, although several were exposed to terrible diseases. But let me introduce this gallant little army, whose exploits and impressions comprise so much of this book:

Howard Baer:—Assigned as an artist war-correspondent to the Burma-India-China theatre, where he produced fifty-five paintings and sketches.

Baer was born in a little mining village near Pittsburgh in 1907. He received his art education at Carnegie Institution. You perhaps know him as cartoonist and illustrator for such magazines as Esquire, the New Yorker and Colliers, for it wasn't until 1941 that he finally gave way to a great urge to paint. His assignment in the Orient took him into the heart of the Burmese jungle where he was with General Stilwell's forces and with Merrill's Marauders during the fighting to reopen the Burma Road. He saw India and spent considerable time in China with the Allied troops. Baer is represented in the permanent collections of numerous museums, including the Metropolitan.

Robert Benney:—Assigned to the Western Pacific Theatre and did thirty-one paintings and sketches.

Benney is a native New Yorker and was born in Brooklyn in 1904. He studied art at Cooper Union, the Art Students League and the National Academy of Design. His portraits of famous contemporary American actors have been exhibited at the New York Public Library and the Museum of the City of New York. He first gave full time to painting in 1936-37 while doing an extensive tour of the West Indies and South America. The work which he produced during these travels, and on the Gaspé Peninsula, Canada, was shown at national art exhibitions throughout the United States.

Peter Blume:—Assigned to do a painting at the great Halloran General Hospital, on Staten Island, New York.

Blume was born in Russia in 1906 and was brought to the United States when he was five years old. He began art studies at the age of twelve in public school night classes. Later he studied at the Educational Alliance Art School. In 1934 he received the coveted Carnegie International Award, and was one of the youngest American artists ever to get this honor. He also was given the Guggenheim Fellowship, 1932-36. He is represented in the Metropolitan Museum and in numerous others.

Franklin Boggs:—Assigned to the Southwest Pacific Theatre. Eighteen paintings and sketches.

Boggs was born in Warsaw, Indiana, thirty-one years ago and already has achieved an important place in contemporary American painting. He was awarded two European traveling scholarships from the Pennsylvania Academy of Fine Arts, as well as its first Toppan award in 1940. In 1940, too, the Tennessee Valley Authority invited him to make drawings and paintings which would depict the vast conservation and power activities of this major project for public information. His paintings have been exhibited in many leading museums. During his Pacific assignment he witnessed four important actions.

Howard Baer

Robert Benney

Peter Blume

Franklin Boggs

Francis Criss:—Assigned to Army Medical Center, Washington. Seven paintings.

Criss was born in London in 1901 but came to this country as a child and his work has been closely identified with America. He holds the unusual honor of having won three major fellowships for the study of painting—a four-year scholarship in the Pennsylvania Academy of Fine Arts, the Cresson Scholarship for study in Europe, and the Guggenheim Fellowship for study abroad. He studied at the Graphic Sketch Club in Philadelphia, and later at the Pennsylvania Academy of the Fine Arts and at the Art Students League in New York. He has been given exhibitions both in this country and abroad by important museums, many of which own his work, as do several leading private collectors.

John Steuart Curry:—Assigned to the Army Medical Department training school at Camp Barkeley, Texas. Twelve paintings.

Curry was born on a Kansas farm in 1897. By the time he was thirty-one he had studied in several art institutes both in America and abroad. He won his first public recognition when his "Baptism in Kansas" was shown at the Corcoran Gallery in Washington. This picture later was acquired by the Whitney Museum. He has murals in the Department of Justice and Department of Interior buildings, Washington, in the Kansas State Capitol and in the University of Wisconsin. He is artist-in-residence at that university.

Ernest Fiene:—Assigned to plants of medical industry on the home-front. Ten paintings.

Fiene was born in the Rhineland in 1894. In the course of his studies he attended the National Academy of Design and the Art Students League. Twice he returned to Europe for study, the first time in France and England, and later on a Guggenheim Fellowship for work in Italy. Fiene's works have won several prizes at major exhibitions, and the Metropolitan Museum of Art and numerous other museums throughout the country own paintings by him. He has murals in the Department of Interior building, Washington, and in other cities.

Marion Greenwood:—Assigned to England General Hospital at Atlantic City, N. J., where men wounded overseas are reconditioned. Twenty-four paintings and sketches.

Miss Greenwood was born in New York City in 1909 and comes from a family of artists. Her grandmother, her father and her sister, Grace, all are painters and her brothers are commercial artists. She studied at the Art Students League in New York, at the Academie Collarosi, Paris, and in Mexico. When she was only twenty-three she became the first American woman to paint a mural for the Mexican Government, and received public praise for her work from former President Cardenas. Later she did murals for Mexico City Civic Center, as well as for buildings in various parts of the United States. Miss Greenwood has exhibited her paintings widely, and has lectured on painting at Columbia and several other schools.

Joseph Hirsch:—Assigned to the Mediterranean Theatre, Italy. Twenty-two paintings and sketches.

Hirsch comes from Philadelphia, where he was born in 1910. He has had a brilliant career and has been showered with many honors. He studied in the Pennsylvania Museum School of Art, being graduated with two first prizes. Other awards include the Woolley Fellowship by the Institute of International Education for travel in Europe, the Third Hallgarten prize by the National Academy of Design, the Walter Lippincott prize for the best figure painting in oil by an American at the Pennsylvania Academy's Fine Arts Exhibition, and honorable mention in the Prix de Rome competition. For a year and a half Hirsch traveled through Italy, France, Spain, Belgium, England, Holland, Egypt, Ceylon, China and Japan, studying the art of those countries. His assignment in the Mediterranean wasn't the first of its kind in the second World War, for he previously had served as an artist war-correspondent in the Pacific theatre. His work is owned by leading museums.

Fred Shane:—Assigned to the Army Medical De-

Francis Criss

John Steuart Curry

Ernest Fiene

Marion Greenwood

4

partment training school at Carlisle Barracks, Pa. Fourteen paintings and sketches.

Shane was born in Kansas City in 1906. He studied at the Kansas City Art Institute, Colorado Springs Fine Art Center, and in Paris and New York. He has been the winner of many prizes and awards and his work is represented in museums and private collections throughout the country. His honors include the winning of the MacMillan Purchase Prize from St. Louis City Museum, the Byng Memorial Purchase Prize from Springfield, Mo., Museum, and many awards from Kansas City Institute. He is a member of Missouri University faculty.

Lawrence Beall Smith:—Assigned to the European Theatre—England and France. Eighteen paintings and sketches.

Smith was born in Washington, D. C., in 1909. He is a graduate of the University of Chicago and received his early art training at the Art Institute of Chicago. He has exhibited widely and his work is hung in Harvard University and many other public and private collections. His assignment in Europe included the coverage of D-Day, and he went into Normandy with our troops through a beachhead. That wasn't his first experience with war, however, for he had done painting previously aboard an aircraft carrier.

Manuel Tolegian:—Assigned to the Army Nurse Corps training school at Camp White, Oregon. Ten paintings and sketches.

Tolegian was born in 1911 in Fresno, California, of Armenian parents who emigrated from Angora, Turkey. His father was a famous poet. Tolegian was educated in the University of California and then went to New York to study at the Art Students League.

Among his teachers was John Steuart Curry, whom the reader already has met as one of the artists who did paintings for this book. Tolegian's work is owned by leading museums, and the late President Franklin D. Roosevelt personally selected a Tolegian picture for permanent hanging in the White House. The youthful artist's gifts go outside his painting, for he composed music in the Pulitzer Prize-winning play, Time of Your Life, by Saroyan.

That completes the list of twelve artists who have used their great talent to help us visualize some of the marvels which are performed for our fighting men by the United States Army Medical Department, and to depict the frequently terrible conditions under which this service is rendered. Perhaps the best way to describe the manifold activities of the Department is to say that it is doctor, surgeon, nurse and dentist to Uncle Sam's millions of soldiers and airmen. And like the old-time general practitioner in the country districts, it carries its own equipment about with it.

The Army Medical Department supervises hundreds of hospitals at home and abroad—erects many of them, for that matter—and gives treatment to thousands upon thousands. It's the largest medical organization the United States ever has had.

The Department comprises (to give the approximate figures at the end of the European War) 45,000 doctors—and there are 83 women among them for the first time in history; 15,000 dentists; 2,000 veterinarians; 2,000 sanitarians; 18,700 members of the Medical Administrative Corps; 61 pharmacists; 52,000 army nurses; 1,500 dietitians; 1,000 physical therapists. All these are quite apart from hundreds of thousands of enlisted men who are serving as litter bearers and in first-aid work.

"Medical men follow the soldier and guard his health from the time he is inducted into the army until he is discharged," to use the language of the Department, "and even after he returns to civilian life he is watched and cared for by other government health agencies. Our armed forces are fighting all over the world, in every kind of climate—from the tropics to the Arctic. They have lived and are living among primitive peoples and have been exposed to every known disease under the most difficult field conditions. They have suffered every type of battle wound.

Joseph Hirsch

Fred Shane

Lawrence Beall Smith

Manuel Tolegian

"Yet, in spite of these handicaps, nearly 97 per cent of the wounded who reach hospitals live; and the disease rate in the army is only one-twentieth as high as it was in the last war—the lowest ever recorded in the army—while the health of soldiers in the field is generally better than that of civilians."

Just think of it—all but three per cent of the wounded who reach hospitals live. This achievement is all the more remarkable when one stops to consider that it wasn't until our American Civil War that methods were devised for anything approaching adequate evacuation and treatment of the wounded during combat. And the death rate still remained terribly heavy.

Up to about the seventeenth century the wounded got little consideration in battle. The best they could hope for—if they were too badly hurt to look after themselves—was that a comrade would put them out of their misery with knife or bullet. Indeed, this dispatching of the wounded wasn't confined to that distant time, for in the last war the soldiers of some countries practiced it to a certain extent in cases where there was no hope for recovery of the wounded man and he was dying in agony. Mercy killing was what they called it.

These days things are different for, as Surgeon General Kirk has said, "the survival rate among our wounded at the present time is higher than it has ever been in any army in any war at any time." In short, unless a man is killed outright, his chances of coming through with his life are first class.

It mustn't be thought that these wonders are wrought by our Army Medical Department without hurt to itself. By the time the European war had run its course, the cumulative casualties of the Department, including all branches, had reached distressing totals. They were:

Killed in action—3,061; wounded—14,026; captured—2,034; missing—2,915.

The U. S. Army Medical Department was born during the siege of Boston in 1775, when it was created by the Congress upon recommendation of General George Washington. It was a small beginning—the recognition of a need rather than the provision of anything like adequate means to meet it. The regulations governing the medical service consisted mainly of an order to provide the wounded and sick with fresh straw upon which to lie. Still it was a start, and it has grown with experiences which have ranged from dealing with wounds inflicted by arrows and tomahawks to meeting the problems of the modern high explosive.

The first army hospitalization installation also was made at the request of General Washington. Several large private homes were used for the sick and wounded from the battlefields. The Congress further provided for a matron "to supervise the nurses, bedding, and so forth," and nurses "to attend the sick and obey the matron's orders." Thus was begun our Army Nurse Corps, of which Surgeon General Kirk has said:

"The Army Nurse is the Army Doctor's right hand. Without her the present high standard of health among our soldiers, and the gratifying percentage of recovery of battle casualties, would be impossible."

2

Doctor to the Army

Surgeon General Norman T. Kirk is a straight-backed, wiry concentration of skill, initiative and unbounded energy, as befits his great position as head of the organization which looks after the physical and mental well-being of Uncle Sam's millions of soldiers. Upon him, in the long run, rests the responsibility for everything from a pin-scratch to a terrible shell wound, from heat-rash to typhus, from an imaginary pain to the nervous disorder which we know as psychoneurosis.

At fifty-seven he is as fit as he was when he had the time for his favorite game of polo. He always was a hard-riding, give-'em-hell player, putting into that strenuous sport everything he had, just as he now flings every ounce of his vast energy into his job. He's a fisherman, too, and his ability in other pursuits extends to that, for he actually brings them home. But if you want to know just how alert and skillful he can be, sit in at a poker game with him—but don't let yourself drowse.

They say General Kirk is tough, but I didn't size him up that way. True, he knows what he wants, and he wants what he wants when he wants it. He's efficient himself and demands efficiency in others. He knows what sort of service he ought to get from his subordinates, too, for he's done most of the jobs they do—and done them supremely well.

I wouldn't want to be the subordinate to fail through inefficiency in carrying out one of his orders. But if I needed a friend I should turn to him, for no man with those tiny wrinkles of good nature about his eyes, and the frequent quirk of humor at the corners of his mouth, can really be tough. Anyway, General Kirk greeted me at our first meeting in his private office in Washington with an agreeable smile as he shook hands warmly, and he permitted me to be the judge of how much of his valuable time I should take. He answered all my questions freely in concise, close-clipped sentences which are characteristic of the man. He doesn't waste words.

General Kirk believes that, due to the pressure of war, medical science has progressed fifteen years since the conflict began.

"This war has been a great boon to medicine," he declared.

That might well be taken as the theme for any review of the achievements of the Army Medical Department. The advance in medicine and surgery is one of the marvels of all time.

Our greatest emergency was when the war started. For instance, we had few surgical instruments, the most of which were made in Germany. Thus supplies became an urgent problem, and manufactories had to be started. Another difficulty was personnel—to get enough doctors. We expanded from 1,200 to 12,000—and finally to close to 50,000 at the peak. We got the best surgeons in the world from civil life, and put them in uniform. The dental corps was increased from a mere 300 to some 15,000, and the number of nurses was jumped from 1,000 to well over 50,000. And so it goes, but we have time for only a thumb-nail sketch here.

I asked General Kirk to name the first three of the war's outstanding innovations, and without hesitation he shot back:

"Surgery, the sulfa drugs and penicillin. Surgery is Number One. It isn't drugs that save lives; it's surgery. Drugs supplement the surgery."

Penicillin and the sulfa drugs have reduced the death rate from pneumonia from 24 per cent in the last war to 6 per cent in this. In the treatment of venereal disease penicillin is performing wonders. Syphilis can now be cured in a matter of days instead of months. Gonorrhea can be cured in days instead of weeks.

The General was quick to add other items of outstanding achievement. Ranking high, of course, is plasma, which has so greatly reduced fatalities by overcoming the wound shock that may cause death unless it is dealt with immediately.

Another first-line drug is atabrine, which is better for malaria than is quinine, and has largely replaced the latter drug.

"We've got malaria licked," said the Surgeon General with satisfaction, "and malaria was a worse enemy than the Japs."

Then, of course, there is the new magic insecticide, DDT. This has proved to be an amazingly effective agent in controlling mosquitoes, which carry malaria and other diseases; the fly and other insects which are distributors of dysentery; the common louse, which spreads typhus, the scourge of former wars.

The wonders of DDT were well illustrated in Naples, Italy, where a threatened epidemic of typhus was prevented. Its use in Europe and the Balkans is estimated to have saved millions of lives. It was a godsend to the Pacific theatre, too, where islands like Saipan, which were a mass of flies and mosquitoes, were quickly freed of these carriers of death.

Now when we list all the achievements of the Army Medical Department we are thinking in terms of its two most important functions in wartime— the treatment and evacuation of the wounded. You have to move fast, you know, if you are going to save the life of the soldier who has been struck down on the battlefield. Prompt medical care by highly skilled specialists, together with mobility of medical services in the field (especially evacuation services), contributed to the low mortality rate of only three per cent among the wounded reaching surgical treatment, as against 8.1 per cent in World War I.

How treatment and evacuation combine into a nearly perfect service may best be understood by following an injured soldier through what would be the "normal" chain if everything went according to the book. This would seem to be a good time for the reader to take the trip. It is here that the "Men Without Guns" play such a great part, and we shall be seeing much of their activities just as soon as we hit the battle zones.

When we speak of the "normal" chain, it must be understood that in actual combat virtually everything is more nearly the opposite of normal. This provides the basis for the soldier's odd term of "Snafu," which is the alphabetical contraction for "Situation normal, all fouled up." So, as the Medical Department points out, this "normal" chain is subject to modification at every link to suit the situation. It represents the planned, ideal way of handling the wounded, and is followed as closely as circumstances permit.

The first step when a soldier gets wounded is for him to give himself first aid if he can—and most times he can. Every fighting man is trained in first-aid principles, and he carries with him in battle all the things he may need in such emergency.

Next the wounded man makes his way back to the battalion aid station, which usually isn't more than a few hundred yards from the front line. If he is hurt so badly that he can't help himself, there are medical aid men nearby to administer first aid and carry him to the station. The Department states that a survey made during operations in France revealed that the wounded received aid "right away," the unanimity of that answer making it difficult to fix an average for the time elapsed between being hit and receiving first medical aid.

The medical soldiers, generally known as "medics," remove the wounded to protective covering, give what help they can and then attract the attention of litter bearers before moving on with advancing troops. This first emergency treatment usually consists of giving sulfa drugs or morphine, dressing the wound to prevent hemorrhage, applying splints for fractures, or making tourniquets. Blood plasma is given.

Here I want to break our chain for a moment to tell a little story emphasizing the ubiquity and bravery of the corpsman—that he is indeed on the job unless he himself has been stricken, and that the wounded soldier does get help "right away." This incident involved my colleague John Moroso, 3rd, Associated Press war correspondent.

It was the beginning of the Allied invasion of Sicily—July 9, 1943. In the pre-dawn darkness Moroso was swimming ashore through a storm-swept sea after his landing craft had been wrecked, when he heard a call for aid from the nearby water. The appeal came from an American lieutenant who was drifting helplessly in the waves because of a terribly shattered leg which had been broken as he was leaving his landing craft.

Moroso towed the injured officer up onto the beach-head. Then, in violation of orders forbidding any shouting by the invading forces, the correspondent yelled into the dark: "Medic! Medic!"

Immediately not one but two corpsmen materialized from the inky blackness and took charge. The beach-head was being swept by enemy fire, and the ocean spray was pouring over them, but they went to work. Proceeding without light—since it was strictly forbidden to show any—they set the lieutenant's leg and put splints on it. Mind you, all this was done by sense of touch, with an expertness acquired from being trained to work in the dark. Then they got their man to a small boat which took him to the assault transport Thomas Jefferson. And a doctor said the leg couldn't have been set better aboard the ship.

You can't beat that very much for getting aid "right away."

While we are on the subject of the first-aid man, there's one very intimate thought which I should like to give you here in passing. You'll find it recurring time and again as our story unrolls. The corpsman on the firing line is many things beside first aid to the badly wounded man.

You get the feel of it when you see the boy who is injured clinging to his helper for comfort—like a kid turning to his mother when he has been hurt. And you get it even more poignantly when, in the great emergency, you see the corpsman kneeling and saying a prayer as the GI slips away on his last journey.

But to get back to our wounded man who is going through the chain from the battlefield. After the first-aid treatment, the litter bearers carry him to the battalion aid station. Much of this litter work is done under fire. At the battalion aid station doctors take charge and decide whether he shall be returned to combat or moved along the chain of evacuation to the collecting station. If his injuries are minor he is given further treatment, a rest, and is returned to the front. If he needs more treatment he is moved by ambulance, jeep or litter to the collecting station, which may be a few hundred or several thousand yards from the front.

If the wounded man still requires treatment he next is passed on to the clearing station, which is a temporary but well-equipped hospital. Here he may remain several days until he can be moved again, either back to the front or to the next medical stop. These clearing stations usually are operated in pairs so that they can leap-frog to keep up with the advancing troops. Normally each is staffed by 12 doctors and 96 enlisted men.

Some 12 to 15 miles to the rear—in some cases as much as 50 miles—is the evacuation hospital to which the wounded man goes from the clearing station. This evacuation hospital is provided with all the equipment of a modern hospital, and here major medical or surgical needs are attended to.

The next big link in the chain is a general hospital. This is a fixed installation providing general medical and surgical care. From the general hospital our man goes to an embarkation hospital, and is moved by hospital-ship or hospital-plane to the homeland. There he is landed at a debarkation hospital where he remains only long enough to be routed to an appropriate general hospital—as near his home as possible.

Then his treatment and rehabilitation are carried on to fit him for his re-entry into civilian life. All the skill which the medical profession and makers of surgical appliances have learned in this war is brought into play to restore our wounded man as near to normal as is humanly possible. But more of this period of rehabilitation in a later chapter.

It will be clear that these many services—from the firing line to the general hospital at home—require a vast business organization to handle the supply of medical and technical personnel and of equipment and drugs. Here is where Deputy Surgeon General Lull takes the stage.

General Lull, like General Kirk, is efficient. On his broad shoulders falls the mountainous task of procurement of personnel and supplies, and the building and equipment of hospitals. It's his business, too, to keep the service around the world informed of new overall policies for treatment of patients.

The story of medical supplies is in itself one of the great chapters of the war history. Just as military strategy tries to leave nothing to chance, so the Medical Department specifies, tests, buys, stores, and ships all over the world hundreds of thousands of items in anticipation of needs.

The Department states that for medical supplies and equipment alone, the Service Forces spent $802,-803,929 in the fiscal years 1943 and 1944. That figure doesn't include the cost of maintenance, transportation and operations. All told, the Department buys about 12,000 different items, and these range from surgical instruments and drugs to prefabricated buildings.

A sensational example of the gigantic proportions of the supply and personnel problem is seen in preparations for care of the wounded on Normandy D-Day, June 6, 1944. Of course, Heaven was good to us and our casualties were far less than had been prepared for, but here is the way the Medical Department was set for this great adventure as the result of many months of labor:

Fixed hospital beds to the astonishing number of 97,400 were ready in Army hospitals in England, and provision was made for accommodation of 196,-000 patients by full use of previously surveyed locations of hospital units. These could have been staffed with doctors—including such specialists as internists, surgeons, psychiatrists, radiologists and orthopedic surgeons—nurses and enlisted personnel within 24 hours if the emergency required.

Only necessary beach installations and port construction to insure the flow of supplies into the zone of operations took precedence over care of the wounded. Hospitals had first priority in construction work.

If casualties had exceeded expectations, plans were made for evacuation from the United Kingdom by air and ship to the United States.

There were waiting in England—not including staffs of battalion aid stations, collecting stations and evacuation hospitals to be landed in Europe—8,000 doctors, more than 10,000 nurses, 1,600 dentists and more than 100,000 trained medical and surgical technicians ready to take care of the wounded.

The following supplies were stored and ready for use: 800,000 pints of blood plasma; 600,000 doses of penicillin with 600,000 more ready for shipment in July; 10,000 pounds of sulfa drugs; 650,000 morphine syrettes (½ grain each); adequate supplies of anesthetics; more than 2,000,000 surgical instruments; 2,000 doses of tetanus toxoid (for booster shots following a wound), and 8,000,000 first-aid packets.

Fifteen hospital ships, not including LST's and other small craft, were used in surface evacuation from France to England. As soon as air strips were secured, fifty planes, each capable of carrying eighteen patients, began shuttle service for the wounded across the Channel.

You'd think that such a mighty undertaking, the greatest of its kind ever envisaged, represented the last word in complexity, but the problems of providing the best and swiftest medical care for our men in the Pacific theatres of combat were even more difficult. There hospitals had to be transported much greater distances by water, and then overland by trucks.

Operating rooms for such theatres are on wheels. Specially constructed hospitals, dismantled and packed so they can be carried on men's backs, are quickly reassembled and set up wherever a site is found. The wounded are evacuated mostly by air because there are no roads and most transportation is done with oxen and mules.

Virtually all supplies also are brought in by air to the jungle zones of combat. Evacuation hospitals usually are set up right on the beaches.

These are just a few of the high-spots in the amazing story of the Army Medical Department's achievement in providing the multiplicity of supplies needed for the care of our fighting men—by far the best care the world ever has known. One could fill a library with the details, but we must hasten to the actual battlefields. Before we embark on this adventure, however, there is one more department which the reader should meet—the great Army Nurse Corps.

All nurses in the Army now are Army nurses—members of the Army Nurse Corps—having the status of officers. The Second World War has taken them to service in every part of the globe, and they have made a glorious record of devotion and heroism. They have carried their life-saving from Iceland to the steaming jungles. They have followed our troops onto beach-heads within a matter of hours after the invasion. Some of these brave girls have been killed, some wounded, some captured, and some of them are missing. They have kept their bond, which is the pledge of the Army Nurse:

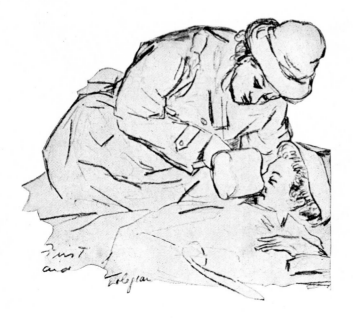

"As an Army nurse I accept the responsibilities of an officer in the Army Nurse Corps.

"I shall give faithful care to the men who fight for the freedom of this Country and to the women who stand behind them.

"I shall bring to the American soldier, wherever he may be, the best of my knowledge and professional skill.

"I shall approach him cheerfully at all times, under any conditions I may find.

"I shall endeavor to maintain the highest nursing standards possible in the performance of my duties.

"I shall appear fearless in the presence of danger and quiet the fears of others to the best of my ability.

"My only criticism shall be constructive. The reputation and good name of the Army Nurse Corps and of the nursing profession shall be uppermost in my thoughts, second only to the care of my patients.

"I shall endeavor to be a credit to my Country and to the uniform I wear."

The Superintendent of the Army Nurse Corps is Colonel Florence Blanchfield, one of the remarkable women of our time—the right woman in the right place. In her fine eyes burns the idealism of the nurse's pledge.

Her experience has been great, including eighteen months as a nurse with American troops in Europe during the first World War. In the Hitlerian conflict she visited England, Belgium, France, Holland, Luxemburg, Germany and Italy in pursuit of her duties as head of the Nurse Corps. And she went where she could see what was going on. She was in Aachen, for instance, soon after that badly shattered German city was captured by our forces.

I found Colonel Blanchfield intensely interesting as we talked in her office at Army Medical Department headquarters. Here are some of the highlights of what she told me:

"Our nurses are actuated by the ideal of service.

"There's no glamour about nursing. Unless you want to help others and make sacrifices, you have no right to be in nursing.

"A nurse must adapt herself to conditions on the battle front. The type of work in this war is far different from that of the last, and it calls for much greater fortitude and sacrifice. In the first World War the nurses were in the rear areas, but this conflict has demanded that medical installations move with the army, so the nurses go up with the army.

"Some of the forward nurses are as far up as the clearing stations (normally from four to seven miles behind the front line and a highly dangerous position). You have to care for your patient where he is. He can't be brought to the nurse.

"It has amazed folk that the nurses could adapt themselves to such conditions. But not one nurse complained to me when I was overseas. So long as they are serving their patients, they are happy. None of the girls in advance areas wanted to go back to the rear echelons.

"This reaction is the outstanding point of the Army Nurse Corps in the war.

"Every nurse is a volunteer. She is nursing because she wants to. Weak spots showed up in training and were counted out."

We were closing the interview when the Colonel added a thought which shows her broad understanding and her solicitude for the women under her.

"Don't forget the girls back home," she said. "Nurses' services are equally important wherever they are. They don't like to be idle. Those who are serving at home rather than at the front are good soldiers in every respect, adjusted to all situations.

"Work at home is just as important as at the clearing station. There is the same consecration to duty at home."

The significance of Colonel Blanchfield's remark that "weak spots showed up in training, and were counted out" is seen in the tough schooling the girls get. This is well summed up by Artist Manuel Tolegian in his comment on the training which he studied at Camp White, Medford, Oregon.

"The war consciousness superseded every other consideration," he told me. "This was war and the training emphasized it at every turn."

Tolegian depicted these young women sweating it out under realistic combat conditions which included all the difficulties and hardships of the front-line. Certainly "weak spots" would show up under this rigorous program if ever, but the artist found seriousness and efficiency the outstanding characteristics.

This intensive training is, of course, typical of the entire Army medical structure. The grilling of officer-candidates, for example, is a really terrific test of physical stamina and ability to "take it." That's very natural, for if competent medical officers could be created by the simple expedient of putting uniforms on doctors, then there wouldn't be any need of an elaborate Army Medical Depart-

ment. The medical officer is a specialist in the unusual emergencies which arise from war.

The Medical Department operates two principal officer-candidate schools. One is the Army Service Force Training Center, at Camp Barkeley, Texas, and the other is the Medical Field Service, Carlisle Barracks, Pa. These schools respectively are dealt with pictorially in this book by Artists John Steuart Curry and Fred Shane.

The primary quality sought among applicants in these schools is proven leadership capacity, and the training they get certainly brings out all their capabilities. Students are put through all phases of actual field operations, staged by bodies of regulars which are stationed at the schools for that purpose.

Just as in actual battle, "wounded" men (labeled according to their supposed condition) are picked up, perhaps given "blood plasma" and "morphine," bandaged and rushed to the hospital. "Battles" rage day and night, and often the corpsmen are working in pitch dark.

There are "gas" attacks, and Fred Shane told me that at Carlisle Barracks they even had a "German" prisoner, outfitted in German uniform, who was "wounded." Corpsmen bandaged his hurt and then brought him in for questioning, just as would have happened on the real battle front.

Highly important are special tests which call for improvisation. In this manner are the students taught to think beyond their "book learning" in meeting the many emergencies of the battle zone. And they do meet the unusual situations when thrown on their own. Because they are young and energetic, they have developed new ideas by their experiments under pressure of necessity.

Apropos of this general thought it can be recorded that Army surgeons have been able to call attention to new enemy weapons by the type of wound or burn. Some of the first tips have come from these quick-thinking specialists who have adapted themselves to the environment of war at close quarters.

3

Southwest Pacific

The nature of the war in the Pacific is well characterized by the fact that the Allies in the main were compelled to abandon the use of the Red Cross for protective purposes in saving life, because a barbaric enemy used this emblem of mercy as a target for bombs and bullets.

Not only was it necessary for Uncle Sam's forces to obscure the Red Cross on hospitals, but the first-aid man early learned to smear mud over insignia on his ambulance and to remove his armband as he went about his rescue mission on the battlefield. Many a hospital had been bombed, and many a corpsman had fallen to a bullet, before the Americans learned the manner of enemy they were fighting.

Typical of Japanese tactics was the savage attack on the United States hospital ship Comfort, loaded to capacity with wounded, off Okinawa on April 28, 1945. A Japanese suicide pilot dove his plane into the Comfort, killing some 29 people, including five Army Medical officers and six Army nurses. The attack was deliberate. It was delivered in bright, full moonlight after the pilot had made several runs.

The problems of the Pacific fighting were many. Much of the warfare, of course, was in the jungles where the enemies which our men encountered included fierce heat and horrible diseases, insects which carried death, and horrors like land-crabs and huge rats. In many instances these things were worse than the enemy bullets.

It is a marvel that our death lists in the Pacific weren't larger. The answer is that while the toll of wounded was heavy, the Medical Corps saved most of these men.

It was into this savage and most far-flung war of history that Artist Franklin Boggs was sent early in 1944 to paint scenes which you see in this book. He was assigned to the American invasion of the Admiralty Islands.

This group had been governed by Australia under mandate from the League of Nations, the islands formerly having belonged to Germany. The Japanese occupied the Admiralties early in 1942 and used them as a valuable refueling station on the routes southward from their great naval base of Truk, 750 miles northeast. Rabaul, the Nipponese base in northeastern New Britain, lay 350 miles to the southeast of the Admiralties, and the strong

enemy base of Wewak on New Guinea was 275 miles to the southwest. So it can be seen that the Admiralties were a real prize.

In recognition of this, on February 29, 1944, an American fleet bearing troops thrust daringly across the Bismarck Sea and invaded the Admiralties in a surprise attack directed by General Douglas MacArthur from the bridge of a warship. Our men landed on Los Negros isle, just off the northeastern tip of Manus which is the principal member of the group. Then on March 15 we drove on to Manus itself under the protection of broadsides from Yankee destroyers. By the following day the strategic airport of Lorengau was in our hands and our position in the Admiralties was secure. But I want Boggs to tell you his own story, and this is the way he related it to me:

I was assigned to the Southwest Pacific. When I arrived in Australia it was suggested that I see the base hospitals first. It was thought that if I saw the front lines first other things would seem tame to me. So in Melbourne and Sydney and Brisbane I visited the big base hospital centers.

Each one of these hospital units was different. For instance, the one at Melbourne was made up of Cleveland doctors, and near Brisbane there was a Harvard group. There were separate hospitals with specialists in certain things, such as bone surgery and skin grafting.

At Gatton there was a rehabilitation center and there they took men who were wounded and reconditioned them to be put back into the lines again to fight. Their morale wasn't too hot. These fellows had suffered from malaria and they felt that they had done their turn. War brings out the good and bad. You are taking a cross-section of American manhood. There were fellows who didn't fit into the army in the first place. Some tried to get out of it.

(In thus referring to malingering, Boggs cites a condition which exists in every army, in every war theatre—and has existed for time immemorial. It is one of the problems which all nations have to face, but the reader should not fall into the error of thinking that malingering was widespread among the American forces, for it was not. However, since the Medical Corps encountered it in most theatres, it is well that we take note of it.)

The men (malingerers) complained of having chronic stomach trouble, or what not. The medics had so much difficulty trying to take care of the wounded that they couldn't always look after these special cases, so they sent the complainers back to the base hospitals. There a diagnosis was made and they were treated.

The doctors would discover that there was nothing the matter with a guy. He was shipped up to the front again. He pulled the same thing once more. Some of the men came back two or three times. It was really quite a problem. Generally there was nothing the matter with them—they were professional "gold bricks."

There were malaria cases that were discharged because they were chronic. There was a rule that no one who had malaria could leave the theatre. Many of the men were taking atabrine pills (the famous new malaria medicine) and they would hide them. They would get malaria on purpose in order to stay out of the fighting. The doctors would line these fellows up, as you see in my picture of men taking pills (the title of this picture is "Pill Call"),

and made sure they took them. These pills turn you to about the color of a lemon.

About this time the Admiralty Islands campaign began. This was the first move north of New Guinea —an amazing place where there are large mountains 13,000 feet high. At that time they were doing some fighting at Saidor but it wasn't heavy and I had to go where it was.

I flew over the Coral Sea from Australia to Port Moresby (southeast New Guinea). Out in the Coral Sea it was beautiful—coral reefs down below. The colors were like jewels—green and blue and gray and white. Generally the corals are submerged. Sometimes they look like doughnuts underneath the water. From Port Moresby I worked my way to Finschhafen where there was an airstrip which had been carved out of the jungle. Fighter planes were taking off all the time. They were just like bees.

The invasion of the Admiralties was in full force and we already had captured Momote (on Los Negros Island just east of Manus) from the Japanese. I went into Los Negros. You could see the Japanese fighting through the smoke.

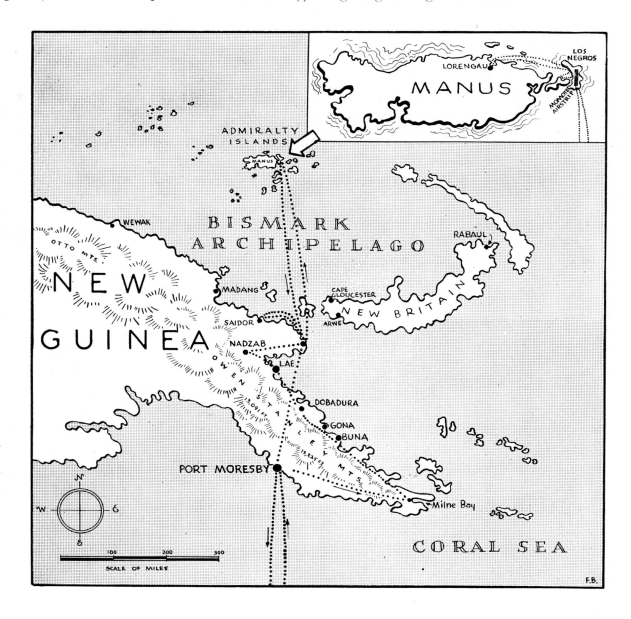

There were a lot of our ships unloading, and supplies were lined up along the beach. There were many jeeps and trucks hauling these things away. They really had got a good hold of the airstrip.

I told Colonel John Hall (Army Medical Corps officer) that I wanted to get real fighting in the front lines. He said:

"Let's go!"

"Do you have someone to go along with me?" I asked.

"I will go with you," he replied.

We started out in his jeep and he took me to a place called Papatali Mission. There had been a mission at that place and the Japanese had taken over. Our fellows had made a landing on this particular spot the day before and 300 men who had pushed up through the dense undergrowth had been caught in enemy cross-fire.

I did a painting of three battalion aid stations. On D-Day at Los Negros Colonel Hall set up an emergency operating room in a former Japanese pillbox. (From this Boggs made his picture "Battalion Aid Station.")

While we were up at Papatali Mission an officer told Hall he was afraid one of the outfits had been cut off because communication had been lost. Somehow the Japanese had cut the Signal Corps lines.

"We have got to get up there," said Hall.

That man deserves a lot of credit. He is a courageous guy.

We got into a little old rowboat and some Australians rowed us down along the coast to a point where we landed. We started up inland with some native ammunition carriers. We didn't know where the Japs were. Suddenly there was an ungodly scream and everybody fell flat. One of the natives told us it was a jungle bird. On we went to what had been a Jap outpost. There was rice and stuff all over the place. It was very smelly. We had a little rest there before going up.

It was really quite dramatic. Along this trail we met a fellow sitting with a tommy-gun. He was an outpost to check and see what went on. We met some Signal Corps fellows stringing wire, followed by a chap with a tommy-gun.

We passed a group coming down this trail. One of our men called out:

"Hey, what happened to Mike?"

"He got it," replied the other.

"Is he dead?" our man asked.

"Not yet," was the laconic answer.

Then there was silence.

We arrived on the top of the hill where the battalion aid station was. There was a medical captain in charge of this station and he had three doctors besides first-aid men. They had lost some of these aid men who had crawled out to get the wounded.

Natives carried down the wounded. The native labor was called Angau, which stands for Australia New Guinea Administrative Unit. There were 30,-000 employed in the New Guinea campaign and through Lend-Lease some of these fellows worked for us. General MacArthur paid them a tribute when he said it would have been impossible for the New Guinea campaign to succeed without them.

Colonel Hall went about checking what the Medical Corps needed. He wasn't supposed to be out in the field doing this kind of work but he did it to make sure things were going properly. He told the fellows off, too, if everything wasn't all right. He risked his neck—a fighting fool—and they admired him.

During our trip we stopped at every battalion aid station along the coast. They had an arrangement whereby the wounded were evacuated from these stations in barges and were taken to a hospital which had better facilities. This set-up was amazingly efficient.

The battalion aid stations, which accompany the troops, treat for shock and bandage wounds. If a man was dying, they would take a chance and perform a major operation, but generally a battalion aid officer is a specialist in first-aid treatment and in putting splints on fractures. He must know what to do quickly in order to keep the wounded man in condition until he can be sent back to a hospital.

I went over to Manus Island and it was amazing what the war was like on a beach-head. You think of constant fighting but it's not like that. There was artillery set up on an island two miles off shore to knock out the Japs and it was firing over our heads as we came in. Supplies were being unloaded, and there were fellows in swimming, having a wonderful time while the guns boomed. Wounded men were coming in—one with his jaw shot and hanging down.

We pushed in from the beach a little way to a hill. The Japanese had heavy guns but our men had swarmed up to the crest. One of the wounded bound for the battalion aid station had been shot through the leg and was in agony. I had a camera along with me and when he saw this he begged me not to take his picture looking like that. Many of the men were overcome by the heat in the fighting, and four had passed out from exhaustion. The Admiralty Islands are only about two degrees short of the equator.

On the way back from the beach-head the boys who were in charge of the landing-barge wanted to know what I was doing, and I explained that I was on assignment for the Army Medical Corps. They were in sympathy with the corps and everyone thought that it was doing a swell job. These men didn't even know what month it was or what day it was. The chief thing running through their minds was "When do I get home?" It was a job to be done.

The corpsmen and the GIs were constantly asking questions about their comrades—"Have you seen so-and-so?"—"How is he?"—"How many fellows are out there wounded?" When a wounded fellow is brought into the battalion aid tent they talk together just as though they were discussing a football game. "Mike got it when that mortar shell hit"—"That machine-gun opened up right in front of my face."

It's astonishing that more lads were not killed. The Japs felt that they were going to die anyway and might as well take down a couple of their enemies with them.

Back in Los Negros they had set up an operating room, 30 by 80 feet. Four operating tables were going constantly. There were about five or six surgeons, all young fellows, and I went in at night when they were operating.

There was no picture of men in white. I think in Europe it might have been a little different but out there these medics had to contend with the rains, and the water came into their operating theatre. It was muddy, and there were bloody bandages about. The surgeons wear only a pair of shorts and a little operating cap.

I saw one fellow—a very handsome young lad—having his leg amputated. He didn't know what had hit him, because he was knocked out when a piece of mortar shell struck him. As he lay there naked on the operating table you wondered what thoughts would go through his mind when he came out from under the anesthetic.

One of the most dramatic things that I saw was a corpsman walking out of a tent, carrying a bucket with an amputated foot in it, and part of a hand and gauze—just a lot of blood and mess. He was going to bury it. That's one of the many duties of the corpsman—that and scrubbing the blood off the stretchers. (This is shown in Boggs' painting "End of a Busy Day," where the stretchers are being cleaned in the surf, for it is said that salt water is good.)

The corpsman who washes the stretcher does a lot to make the wheels of the Medical Corps turn. Some of the men work themselves to death. Probably in civilian life they were meek and mild fellows, and being so close to wounded men they feel that they can't give enough.

For instance, if there's heavy fighting the corpsman never lets up. He has to go right back and get another injured man. He never can say "I'm tired." The enemy snipers pick off a GI. Maybe he's just wounded but is so badly hurt that he can't even crawl from the spot where he has fallen. He yells for help—for water. Along comes a corpsman, and he's a perfect target for some sniper.

If a corpsman has to crawl out to get a wounded soldier, a machine-gunner goes along with him. The corpsman risks his life to get the injured man but knows that his comrade with the machine-gun will avenge any sniper's bullet. I think the corpsmen deserve tremendous credit.

Ice is important in the tropics. In many cases it is used to keep down infection. For instance, if they had been able to get ice they might have saved the leg of that boy who was operated on at Los Negros. With ice available they could have packed his leg and flown him back to New Guinea.

I returned to New Guinea on a B-17 which brought in a cargo of medical supplies and carried wounded men back. They put the patients through the gun turrets to get them into the plane. Only cargo planes are equipped with racks for evacuating the wounded, so these fellows had to be put on the catwalk through the center of the B-17. When we took off it seemed as though we must hit the palm trees on the runway because of the great wingspread of this huge bomber.

With the gun turrets opened there was a great deal of wind coming in and the blankets would blow from the wounded fellows. It was important to keep them covered. A special corpsman went along with the boy who had his jaw shot off. I had followed this case from the day he was wounded. He was all bandaged up, and the fluid from his salivary glands kept running down and choking him. The corpsman went along to keep this GI's head turned and mop his face.

Of course the wounded man couldn't talk. The corpsman would lean over him and ask him if he wanted anything. The GI would reach up and hold the corpsman down to him. He didn't need anything, but he wanted someone near him.

There were tough gunners on this ship sitting on ammunition boxes. They would watch and say, "My God, this is awful!" In looking out for the wounded men, we nearly lost the whole plane. We were about 15 minutes away from the base when a Jap bomber, out on a reconnaissance flight, flew over us and dropped two bombs in an attempt to hit our B-17. One bomb went forward and the other went aft, and our gunners opened up with their 50's but he was too far away.

When I returned to New Guinea there was no place for me to stay except in the ward of a portable hospital with wounded men. I was three beds away from the fellow who had his jaw shot off.

This portable hospital was right in the jungle. It was screened in and had an iron roof on it. In the Pacific you always slept under mosquito nets, which were a sort of green color.

It was a strange experience, being inside a net with a flash-light shining on the scenes about you. A nurse came through to look after a shipwrecked sailor who had swallowed so much oil that he vomited constantly and couldn't keep down food or water. You would see an arm in a cast, or bandaged limbs, sticking up in the air. Men were restlessly turning over.

Outside in the jungle at night there are the damnedest noises. Among other things there is a tropical bird which has a terrible scream. While I was in the Admiralty Islands, everyone had slept with his knife in his hammock. So I figured that I was going to sleep with my knife in the portable hospital. I had my knife right handy and had dozed off when there was a terrific racket on the corrugated iron roof. I grabbed my knife and yelled. Somebody said:

"All right, buddy. Take it easy. Don't get excited. It's just a coconut falling on the roof."

In New Guinea and all the other islands out there conditions had been primitive before the war. There was nothing but native villages, and bringing in nurses was difficult. Consequently nurses didn't arrive until things had been pretty well consolidated. The minute the base hospitals were set up, the nurses came along. In the matter of the Philippines and Saipan the nurses went in sooner because they had buildings as base hospitals and there was less chance of being overrun by the enemy. The Flight Nurses would go on planes to advance bases and come out with the wounded. They did a great job. At Port Moresby, New Guinea, there was the 171st Hospital and this had modern equipment.

One of the terrible diseases of the New Guinea jungle is "scrub typhus." There is a grass called kunai which grows five or six feet high. In that grass there is a louse which breeds typhus germs and infects humans.

This typhus isn't like the European variety. Generally a man will become paralyzed. The paralysis hits him on the seventh day, starting in his legs and working up to his lungs. He gets so paralyzed you would think that he was never going to breathe again, and if he isn't cured by the twelfth or thirteenth day, he is gone. This scourge was all through New Guinea. Our troops were ordered to tie their pants legs and keep their bodies covered as much as possible.

Skin diseases are severe afflictions out in New Guinea and other steamy hot islands of the Pacific. Some of them consist of itchy scaling patches with open sores partly caused by the scratching. Sometimes they spread over the entire body. The soldiers have coined the word "jungle rot" for all types of skin diseases which occur in jungle areas. The doctors don't like this term because it means so many different things. One soldier who writes home and says that he has "jungle rot" might have ordinary athlete's foot, another a skin ulceration, another a dermatitis due to plants, etc. However, soldiers like vivid terms and they won't give up this one. I saw plenty of skin diseases in New Guinea and back in the hospitals of Australia.

The fighting men have to live like rats in the first few days of an invasion. They live in dirt—in the ground. They can't wash their clothes. Because of constant rain and perspiration in intense humidity, their clothes never are dry. Insects get on them and the men start scratching. The men scratch this dirt into themselves and get their skin infected. The first stage produces running and crusty sores. Then come blisters which break, and the infected water spreads to other places. I saw cases where the doctors put piping over the beds to hold up the sheets so that they wouldn't touch the affected men. In some cases the scaling, oozing patches get into the ears and around the eyes and they want to scratch themselves all the time. Skin diseases are bad out in New Guinea, but luckily they are not contagious and the men don't infect each other and they won't infect other people when they come home.

Sometimes the doctors paint the fellows with gentian violet. I was very much impressed. Out in the jungle they had Medical Corpsmen set up a dispensary. Men with sores on their body would go there and corpsmen would paint them with gentian violet. Some of them with a strong sense of humor made their painting with a design. I called one of my pictures "Easter Egg."

One of the most efficient developments in the Army Medical Department operations in the Southwest Pacific was the formation of the portable hospital units, since these units were used in the early stages of invasion. They moved them by man-power through the jungles and they actually transported 24-bed hospitals right over the Owen-Stanley range of mountains in New Guinea. Medical supplies were packed in oil drums which were slung between two poles with straps. The members of the unit had to carry their own food and water for the trip. They moved fast and there seemed to be no place they couldn't go.

Portable units went into the Admiralties on D-Day. The units were so arranged, with prefabricated equipment, that they could be set up and get to work immediately they hit a beach-head. These hospitals had full equipment and were sort of combined battalion aid stations and clearing stations. They not only may be on the firing line, but they also operate. You find them in the jungle, on the beach-heads, and even on the decks of transport ships.

One evening I was walking along a beach. The sun was going out in the west. I saw a blood plasma bottle—a medical first-aid tin broken open—some bloody gauze and torn clothing. These things are symbolic of the Medical Corps. You know that wounded men have been treated. Wherever war has passed, there you see the Medical Corps syrettes.

When we went in and shelled an island it meant that the natives got shelled. Children, who didn't know what it was all about, got hurt. The Army Medical Corps cared for these wounded. One of the doctors at Finschhafen had a beautiful set of native spears as a result of such aid, and the way he got them was this:

There was a very sick little boy in a village. Some natives came to the American hospital and asked this doctor to treat the child. The medic did so, and when the youngster was well his father said to the physician:

"I will give you anything you want."

The medical officer said he would like to have a few spears and arrows. The next day the father brought over a load of them—magnificent ebony fishing spears.

Turning to another phase of the war, I have this feeling: that we are so far away from these boys who are coming back that 90 per cent of the people don't know what the soldiers stand for. We don't know where the places are that they speak of. They talk in GI terms of "jungle rot," and it has no meaning on the home front.

It's going to be very difficult for the average soldier. People won't appreciate what he has gone through and has suffered. Flyers! Folk don't even know what kind of planes the airman has flown. We don't talk the fighting man's language.

While I was at the special hospital at Port Moresby, they had one fellow from Chicago in confinement. He was the mildest-looking man. I took his picture. Well, he had killed three of his fellow fighters at the front when he got so excited that he "blew his top." The authorities found that he had become insane. His recovery is doubtful.

The worst case of this nature was a chap from Oklahoma. He had been a gunman for a racketeer but when the war broke out this trigger-man and two brothers joined the service. They were sent to the Pacific, and his two brothers were killed.

With that the ex-gunman became mentally unbalanced and went AWOL from his labor battalion with a machine-gun. He climbed over the towering Owen-Stanley Mountains and joined up with the Australians on the other side.

I saw the report made on the case by the captain of the Australian unit to which the Oklahoman became attached. This said that he killed 135 Japs. He had no fear whatever but just pursued the enemy with his machine-gun. This idea of exacting vengeance for the death of his brothers became a mania with him and he reached the stage where he was ready to kill anyone.

They got him back to Port Moresby, where they put him in confinement. But he had one of his spells during which he punched a hole through a wall with his bare fists, got out and knocked a nurse down. He knew when his attacks were coming on and used to warn the doctors so that they could handle him during this period. They were afraid that he might never fit into society again because of the possibility of recurrence.

Most of the fellows come out of that sort of thing. I've seen cases of men completely mad, and in about three weeks you wouldn't know that there had ever been anything the matter with them. I saw one lot of heavily bearded fighting men, just back from the front, who were so addled they would sit in a daze. The ship I came back on carried 87 psychoneurotic patients. One fellow jumped overboard. One nurse was out of her mind. Many doctors have lost their reason. This is one of the difficult problems of the Medical Corps.

Here is another impression: We had just had our supper in the Admiralties when a truck called a "hearse" came in. I looked into the hearse and saw a whole row of dead American soldiers. I saw a hand with a high-school ring on it. I saw their bodies taken over to graves.

That sort of thing gets you to thinking. These poor devils out here are fighting this war. They've been taken from their homes. Men will risk their lives. Fighting day after day, life becomes cheap. By the law of averages they feel:

"I will get it sooner or later."

Men do heroic things. None of them think at the time:

"I am doing a brave thing!"

I've seen the greatest affection between two men. I came back on a ship carrying wounded men to the United States. I was interested in a boy who had been hit by a piece of shell and was paralyzed on his right side. He couldn't talk or walk. While he was in the hospital he met a fellow who had a case similar to his own but had recovered.

The fellow who had regained his speech felt that he could help the other by giving him encouragement. He would carry the paralyzed boy in his arms. The Good Samaritan would talk to his buddy and the latter would make answer by shaking or nodding his head. Their greatest fear was that when they got back to the United States they would get separated by being sent to different hospitals.

The men on that ship had been away 26 to 28 months. They had been through the toughest part of the fighting. Coming back home was really something. There were fellows who were unable to walk on deck—and corpsmen carried them up to see the Golden Gate.

"Back from Wewak"   Franklin Boggs 1944

4

Saipan

OUR CONQUEST of Saipan in June and July of 1944 was one of the great battles of the Pacific, for this island not only lay at the crossroads of the Mikado's supply lines but also was a vital stepping stone to Japan proper.

Saipan belongs to the Marianas Group (known also as the Ladrones). It is about 700 miles northwest of Truk—one of Japan's most powerful bases —and some 1,000 miles northeast of the Palau Islands. These three—Saipan, Truk and the Palaus —were names to conjure with in the war against Nippon, for they were towers of Japanese strength and strategy in the Southwest Pacific.

American forces stormed their way onto Saipan June 14 under cover of bombardment by United States warships and the bombing and strafing of carrier planes. The contest for the island was bloody, but by July 9 Admiral Chester W. Nimitz, Commander of all American naval forces in the Pacific, was able to announce:

"Our forces have completed the conquest of Saipan."

Then on July 25 Secretary of the Navy James V. Forrestal reported that American casualties totaled 16,463, including 3,049 killed in action, 13,049 wounded and 365 missing. He stated that more than 5,000 of the wounded already had returned to duty, and added:

"This reduces our net losses at Saipan by about one-third and it speaks volumes for both the morale of the troops and the effectiveness of the Medical Corps."

This Battle of Saipan was the red-hot assignment handed to Artist Robert Benney, and here is the story of his experiences as he told it informally to me:

I went from San Francisco by battleship to Pearl Harbor where I spent several weeks doing base hospital work. Then I was assigned to a transport ship carrying soldiers and marines. You are under strict secrecy when you know where you are going, as all war correspondents do. Once you are aboard ship you can't go back to your hotel.

I spent several weeks on the boat and did lots of work in the sick-bay. Several interesting things happen to the boys on a ship. When you pull out from the home port there is not a thing doing in the sick-bay, but after you are at sea awhile it becomes a well-populated place.

Every fighting unit has its own Medical Corps outfit with it. The men receive regular medical care in the sick-bay. The corpsmen hold constant consultations. They always are trying to improve themselves. The interesting thing is to see the earnestness of the boys to add to their knowledge. They cram and cram and spend hours in the hot ship trying to add to their skill.

That goes on all the time until the troops are ready to go over the side. Each corpsman has a special job. One group is trained in pest control, another for battalion work up front, and still others are litter bearers. They all are specialists. If a boy shows special aptitude in a certain type of work, he will be selected for that. If he is light and agile, and can leap over crags and rocks, he is likely to become a litter bearer. If he is heavier he will be assigned to another job.

My approach was strictly that of observing the average man—to see what happened to the average medical soldier.

The doctors are always on their toes to make sure that the troops are tops all of the time. For instance, the fungus disease in the ears and toes is a common one, and every man who becomes afflicted with this is immediately treated and put back into shape. It is also of the utmost importance to see that all immunization injections are kept up to date.

The cooperation is splendid between the Army and Navy personnel aboard ship. They're completely at the service of one another. The Army takes care of its own men on the trip and the Marines take care of theirs, but the doctors of the two services get together for consultation, and diagnoses are made jointly. The Marine doctor may have been an abdominal surgeon in civilian life. The Navy man may have been a brain specialist. The Army physician may have been a pediatrician. They pool their knowledge.

Our landing on Saipan got underway during the night. Some of the men had to wade quite a distance from their landing craft because the tide had turned. Others went in on ducks (amphibious trucks) and alligators (amphibious tanks). When daylight came it was an amazing sight. Our ships were maintaining a continuous barrage, and we could plainly see our flame throwers smoking out the pill boxes and our carrier planes and ships bombing the heavier Jap installations. There was a great deal of dust in the air, and large smoke columns were pouring from gasoline dumps which had been fired.

Every man had to reach the beach and do his job. You saw pieces of clothing floating on the water. At the outset of the landing you didn't see any dead men. Bodies got caught on the bottoms of amphibious vehicles and showed up days later.

You saw men hauling supplies on the beaches. Everybody was dirty and sweaty and very much the same color—gray. The intense barrage from the ships stirred up the coral dust which covered everything.

There were ducks and alligators taking the wounded back to the ship. My first sight of the wounded was when I saw them being loaded into LCVP's. They had been wounded chiefly by Jap rifle fire and mortars. Some of the first men to land didn't get touched until they had got up on the shore about 100 yards. Then the Japs let them have it.

During and after the landings, numerous ships continually unloaded ammunition and supplies in order to maintain our positions. We pushed the Japs back by weight of materiel and men and tough and bloody fighting.

Each group of Marines and Army men has a certain number of corpsmen to take care of it. The corpsmen "go in" with the fighters. The medics

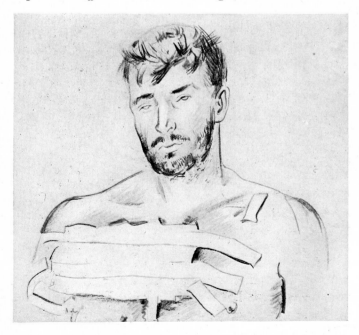

always travel with the troops to which they are assigned. Colonel Elliott G. Colby was the chief surgeon of the Army garrison force on Saipan.

I hitched a ride on a truck which had brought a load of wounded to the beach. The wounded lay in tiers on trucks, and the corpsmen saw that the dressings were in place and gently wiped the injured men's faces and brushed off the numerous flies.

The corpsmen do the same things for these men as their mother would.

It was not quite dark when I finally found my way to the 38th Field Hospital of the 27th Division. The place was littered with wounded. This hospital was located in Chinook Village at the southern tip of the island. To reach it one traveled along the beach road which had but recently been secured. The dust was so thick that you couldn't move more than four or five miles an hour, and the drivers of all trucks and other vehicles were armed against sudden ambush or sniper fire attacks.

Surrounding this village were heights known as "Bloody Ridge" and others from which the Japanese recently had been cleared out but from which snipers still were operating and even shooting patients in the field hospital. Our men have such contempt for the Japanese that they won't use the fox-holes that the Japs have dug, but often dig their own right next to them.

I worked at the 38th Field Hospital, the 31st Field Hospital, the 2nd Marine Hospital, the 5th Amphibious Corps Hospital and at the Clearing and Aid stations. I spent five days and nights at the 33th, sleeping on a litter or on the floor. There was no other place to sleep. The doctors rarely slept. They worked until they either dropped from exhaustion or were ordered off duty. There were slit trenches to dive into when the Japs shelled the area, but these doctors and corpsmen kept on operating during the air raids, working by flashlight at night in the stifling, blacked-out tent.

Along with the surgeons and corpsmen were the Red Cross representatives and the chaplains of the various faiths. These men did a magnificent job, soothing and encouraging the wounded and administering the last rites to the dying. As in my picture "A Prayer for Johnny" (Men with God), at the request of this badly wounded man the chaplain gently reads a psalm while the soldier slowly goes to sleep under an anesthetic.

The wounded men were brought into the receiving tent where they were given plasma in some cases or were taken to the shock tent where almost every man received plasma. The men who drove the jeeps had a tough job, and they looked as though they had been tired for weeks. Frequently these men would work continuously all day, and at night when they got back from the front they would act as litter bearers.

It was eerie the way jeeps loaded with wounded would keep coming down the road at night while Jap planes were approaching. The drivers were supposed to seek cover but they wouldn't desert the wounded. They took the injured men off the jeeps first. For a time there was such a tremendous influx of wounded that there wasn't sufficient tentage for them.

As previously pointed out, the doctors kept right on working during the air raids. From a dugout one night I saw two Jap planes shot down. One exploded into a red ball of flame and fell into Magicienne Bay. I saw men who had been working continually for 24 hours as litter bearers and jeep drivers. They called the jeeps "meat wagons." When the jeep pulled up at night during a raid the drivers would call out "Litter bearer!" and some of these men would crawl from the dugouts and take the wounded into the tent for plasma. I know nothing tougher than leaving a hole during an air raid.

When the Jap bombers were approaching one of the boys would lift the flap of the tent and yell, "Air raid!" Then the switch was thrown for the generator which supplied light for the hospital, plunging the entire area into darkness. Still the operating went on by flashlight. The flap would be lifted again and there would come the yell, "Enemy planes overhead!" Everybody was supposed to stop work and hit the dirt—a regulation which rarely was complied with.

The doctors were completely selfless in their work as the wounded kept flowing in. Sometimes the commanding officer had to order a man off duty because he hadn't slept for such a long time. The Colonel would say:

"This is an order. You must go off duty. You are too valuable to be walking around until you drop."

The doctor then would go into his tent, shave and wash with some of the filthy water in the cistern, lie down for a few minutes—and then get up and go right back to work.

You slept wherever you could find a place but, wherever you were, the infiltrating Japs were apt to discover you. They would crawl up in the darkness and put a grenade by your tent or hut and then sneak away. Snipers would lurk nearby waiting for you to disclose your whereabouts by some movement. One of our doctors was shot in the leg in broad daylight while taking a shower atop a Jap water cistern.

The climate of Saipan is humid and the temperature high. Everybody was wet all the time, and covered with soot and dust. The island is volcanic and everything has to be regarded as highly infectious because of the dust. Every scratch, every wound, had to be treated immediately.

The terrain of Saipan is hilly and jagged and there is jungle on the island. There are numerous insects and pests—scorpions, land crabs, snakes, mosquitoes. The flies from the dead were terrific.

The land crabs would crawl into fox-holes and attack wounded men. There also were plenty of rats which were extremely large.

However, the men stood up very well under all this.

When I hit the landing beach I was stunned for two days. I couldn't do a bit of work. I went into the operating tent and the heat was intense. Every-

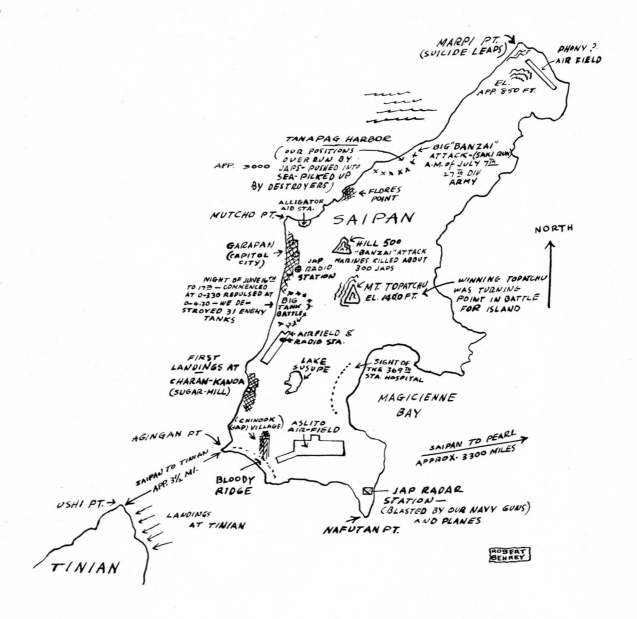

thing was blacked out at night. There was no ventilation. The heat—the smells—the blood—the brain cases! I could take it for 20 minutes or so and then had to go out for air.

The lighting was provided by portable generators. The surgeons usually wore shorts, and sometimes gowns in cases of abdominal or other major operations. They also wore masks.

Our men didn't get gangrene because they had their wounds treated at once, while the natives got gangrene because they had old wounds. The Japs were sent to a separate hospital but they received the same treatment as our men.

(The reader undoubtedly will recognize, without prompting from the writer, that Artist Benney was risking his life every moment of the day and night, just as did the other artists who were assigned to the theatres of war. It was the feeling of these men that it was their duty to collect as much information as they possibly could, even on the firing line,

in connection with the work of the Army Medical Corps. They had to get out and do their jobs and forget about themselves.)

The danger to the medics was the same as it was to the fighting men, and the latter had the highest regard for the corpsmen. Some of the aid stations were no more than slit trenches from which the corpsmen would crawl out, get the wounded and drag them in by a rope tied around them. Once in the trench they could be given plasma.

These slit trenches were in constant danger of being surrounded or overrun by Japs in their banzai charges. The trenches were also under mortar fire on occasion, and a large number of the Medical Corps lost their lives or were wounded.

During the battle the corpsman would crawl out and two riflemen would watch him to keep him covered so that he could get the wounded. If a Jap fired they would pepper his position. In the absolutely silent night they would try to creep up and drop grenades into your fox-hole.

The fighting on Saipan was largely with rifle and mortars. Wherever a line did exist it was taken care of with heavy guns which were going all the time—Bloody Ridge, Hill Five Hundred, Nafutan Point, Agingan Point, Magicienne Bay, Garapan, the battle of Tanapag Harbor.

Marpi Point was where the Jap suicides occurred. The Japanese killed the civilians rather than allow them to surrender. There were three civilian compounds—for Chamorros, Koreans and Japanese— and the civilians poured into the compound by thousands as the battle progressed.

A score or so of Army nurses came in with the Second Echelon after the island was secured. Fighting still continued, however. These girls were put in with the civilian population, and they did a wonderful job. They worked night and day, principally with the women and children of the natives.

In a civilian hospital to which they were attached there was a Japanese girl with a remarkable story. She had been a nurse in civilian life and was in a cave with other civilians and some Jap soldiers when American troops entered to clear them out.

Our men found this girl lying with her throat cut from ear to ear. They rushed her to the hospital and her life was saved. When she was able to talk she explained she had done this because she had been taught that American soldiers always raped women and then killed them. Amazed and grateful for our humane treatment, she gave her services as a trained nurse in the hospital.

A wounded Japanese soldier who was being treated by an American corpsman tried to kill the latter—and this after being bandaged and fed by the Americans. One of the things that the corpsmen in the aid stations and the field hospital had to watch out for was attack by Japanese wounded. If a Jap was sufficiently strong he might seize a knife and attack a doctor.

But to get back to the treatment of our own boys, the shock tent gave you the impression of an assembly line—the men all getting plasma. Some were given five or six units. Some came in there with practically no pulse and appeared quite dead. The doctor would examine the patient and prescribe plasma to be given. Then a corpsman would work on the wounded man, giving him unit after unit, and the strangest sight was to see a man, who had received five or six units, come to life, open his eyes, and ask for a cigarette. He would want to know where he was and would ask if his buddy was all right.

You never heard the really wounded cry out. There was a certain amount of moaning, but no yelling. I heard but one wounded man yell in Saipan, and that was in a hospital area. He was a Jap. He had a superficial wound and thought the Americans were taking him into the tent to torture or kill him.

The corpsmen often would give their blood to the wounded. On the hospital ship Solace a call went out one night for 50 donors, and they got over 250 volunteers from the ship's personnel.

Colonel Colby rode around the island picking hospital sites. Along with his immediate responsibilities his concern was for the future of his men. He really was an artist as well as a great surgeon. He selected his hospital sites after carefully analyzing all the terrain and conditions, looking forward to the rehabilitation period of the wounded with the idea of surrounding them with all the beauty possible, and thereby helping their recovery. He had to do this during battle conditions, projecting his imagination and probing the island for its sensitive beauty in the better days to come.

At Garapan, the capital city, the Japs had a beautiful hospital which we used, of course. Indications were that they had killed all their wounded before they evacuated the place. A captured Japanese medical officer who was questioned as to what the Japanese did with their wounded when they had to retreat, replied that if a wounded man couldn't be evacuated his carotid artery was cut and he was impregnated with an inflammable fluid.

Every wounded or sick American was evacuated by ship or by plane. The first stop back from Saipan was the island of Eniwetok, in the Marshall Islands, where some of the wounded were kept until they were able to continue. We had other hospitals scattered throughout the Pacific islands—Kwajalein, Johnston Island, etc.—where I took notes and made sketches. When the hospital plane landed it was met by a crew which brought up huge blowers that pumped cool air into the plane. Corpsmen fed the

wounded with hot food. All this made it quite comfortable.

On one of the flights with the wounded we carried 15 eye cases. Motor trouble at Johnston Island forced us to wait for another plane, and the wounded men were taken to the hospital. There they were examined immediately and the dressings were changed. The battlefield diagnosis for one of the patients had been total blindness by mortar fragments, but when the doctor took off the bandage he saw that while one eye was dead there was life in the other.

"I think we can give this boy an eye," said the physician.

With that he swabbed the pus from the eye and though it was puffed up and discolored, the eye was O.K. I'll never forget the expression on the soldier's face when he realized he could see again!

This is an example of the Army Medical Corps' vigilance in safeguarding our boys.

5

Italy

ITALY AND other battlefields of the Mediterranean theatre produced some of the most important medical advancements of the entire second World War.

The American Medical Corps—fighting such dread enemies as malaria and typhus, which down the ages had ravaged armies—lost only 585 soldiers to disease from the time of the North African invasion, November 8, 1942, through March of 1945 when the European conflict was rushing to its end. This really amazing record was made public in Rome on May 14, 1945, by Major General Morrison C. Stayer, chief theatre surgeon, whose 50 Army hospitals treated 918,298 members of the United States armed forces during the period in question—and this with a death record of less than one per cent.

One of the early problems of the Army Medical Corps was a malignant type of malaria. In 1943 this was taking the life of one out of every 700 soldiers stricken with it. But by 1944 the ratio had been cut to one in 14,000!

Then there were outbreaks of typhus—that terrible pestilence which is borne by lice—among natives of Africa and Italy, but there were only nine cases in the Army and all of these were non-fatal. For the first time a typhus epidemic was knocked out by a louse powder—the sensational new DDT. This was in 1943 when there was an outbreak of the scourge in Naples and almost the entire population was dusted with this powder.

Bacillary dysentery was kept under control by sulfa drugs. Our sanitation measures were so effective that only 161 cases of typhoid hit the armed forces.

Major General Stayer reported that the doctors of the Mediterranean zone made an outstanding contribution to medical science in the early diagnosis and treatment of jaundice, a disease which hospitalized many American soldiers. He also noted that this theatre pioneered in demonstrating the necessity of adequate, fresh whole-blood for the treatment of shock.

Besides caring for Americans, the Army hospitals also treated Allied fighting men. These included more than 100,000 British, French, Italians, Brazilians, Yugoslavs, Dutch, Poles, Russians, Finns, and Greeks. Then, of course, as in every other theatre, civilians were taken care of when the emergency called for it.

Improvisation, upon which the Army Medical Corps lays so much stress, reached a very high pitch during the Mediterranean fighting. So the story goes.

Artist Joseph Hirsch worked in this zone during March and April of 1944 and brought back a fascinating report to which the writer listened for hours—an account which the reader will see illustrated by Hirsch's pictures in this book. Again I am setting the facts down in the language brought out by a wholly informal conversation—and now Hirsch is speaking:

The outstanding impression of my whole trip was that despite the preparation—and everything apparently is anticipated—yet in the actual zone of fighting things arise which can't be anticipated at all. For instance, they have a wonderful stretcher which is strong, light, can fold up, will hold a 400-pound load, and yet the natives down in the South Pacific (I was in the South Pacific) will get a couple of poles and weave grasses across to make a stretcher. This is springy and a little soft. There is a space between the grass strands and it is cooler and much more comfortable in the tropical climate. The same idea holds good even in the northern zones in summer.

A lot of the things which look medically wonderful on paper, so far as supplies can, didn't cover all the exigencies of actual combat. For example, there is no way in which our Medical Department Supply Service can see to it that a wounded boy on a stretcher is carried down a horribly precipitous rock —not even dirt—at night time, as is shown in one of my pictures. (This painting is called "Night Shift.")

The burden of the Medical Department's job weighs heavily on the men who have to find ways and means—the men at the very front. They have to improvise. All the foresight which is so necessary at Washington still isn't enough. The department makes provision for everything, including front line dental chairs—everything you can imagine! And still the reason it works is because of unique ingenuity.

(The reader will note that Hirsch is emphasizing our old friend, the all-important "improvisation.")

To illustrate: Normally in a back injury—a dislocated vertebra or a broken neck—a boy's whole body has to be kept in traction and very often his entire torso must be incased in a plaster cast. But a dentist in Naples contrived a way of transporting a man with a broken neck in an airplane without a plaster cast.

This dentist had a device which he called a maxillo occipital traction appliance (Hirsch's picture "Medical Ingenuity") by means of which the patient could be transported by litter with the entire body in traction. The pull was maintained by means of an ingenious plate fitting the roof of the mouth. Out of this plate came rods which were connected by rope and pulley to a spring underneath the stretcher. That was a device which was thought of right in the war theatre.

The same dentist got hold of a mine-detector and devised what he called a foreign body locator for shell fragments. A piece of shell would come in any one of many directions and a small wound would be no indication as to where the metal was. The doctor had this little mine detector which instead of being as big as a "pie-plate," like the regular mine, was a three-inch disc with a tiny needle on the oscillation indicator. It would tell where the metal was just as the big detector would locate mines.

Another Army doctor contrived a way of finding a piece of metal in a boy's groin, or ear, or throat, where you can't probe around as you can in a fleshy part. He wired two needles which were inserted into the flesh at approximately right angles. When both needles touched the piece of metal, the circuit was completed and the doctor knew precisely where the fragment was.

To illustrate further, in a field hospital out in the Solomon Islands I saw several notched pieces of two-by-four lumber standing in the corner of a ward and asked what they were. The explanation was that they were used to make a sort of tent frame over beds in case of air raids, the idea of it being this:

When there was a raid all patients who could be moved were immediately taken into a fox-hole. They called even a large air-raid shelter a fox-hole, and very often it was right in the tent. The tents had beds and cots. The latter were light and could be carried very easily but if a badly injured boy was in a heavier bed, the corpsmen made a tent frame over him with the two-by-fours and on this they piled several mattresses. Thus the wounded chap was in his own little air-raid shelter—not very effective with a direct hit but protecting him well in case of a near hit.

Just that simple ingenuity is one of the things where a lack of supplies wouldn't enter into the need for improvisation.

In one hospital there was a sudden rush of patients, necessitating so many changes of sheets that the engineers made a sterilizer out of a gasoline drum with a pressure gauge on it. Thus they had their own little laundry—improvised because the number of patients was so great over the period of a few days. When they brought a boy in, covered with sticky, maroon paste—a combination of his blood and the mud he had lain in—they got hold of some tar paper, spread it on a bed and undressed him there in order to save sheets. The traffic of patients varied so greatly that there was no way in which a doctor could be assured that everything would be there at the right time no matter what happened.

So improvisation is one of the great points to make in connection with the work of the Army Medical Corps—not so much improvising instruments, but improvising ways and means.

I tried to get as much latitude—as wide a variety of corps activity as possible—in Italy. For example, take the veterinary work in the Army.

(This would seem to be a good place for a word of explanation about a highly important but little publicized branch of the Army Medical Department—the Veterinary Corps. It is manned by officers who are graduates in veterinary medicine. The veterinarians have twofold duties: they are responsible for the health of animals in the Army, including horses, mules and war dogs; and they are concerned with the supplies of food of animal origin, which involves an immense job of inspecting and analysis.

(In combat, animals get the same swift treatment as soldiers. Veterinary aid stations receive and record animal casualties, give emergency treatments to disabled animals, return them to duty or prepare them for evacuation. Animals which cannot be salvaged are destroyed.)

The pack mules in Italy were vitally important in the mountainous combat zone. Mules are very sure-footed and sensible. While a horse will get frightened and lose its balance in the dark, these pack mules won't.

Transportation of the wounded was the major problem of the corpsman in the mountain regions. Because the mules wouldn't work on precipitous slopes in the dark, corpsmen very often had to carry the injured back at night. I saw one wounded soldier being transported by eight men. There were four carrying the stretcher, one lugging all their kits, two in front to hold back the little scrub bushes so that the stretcher could pass, and still another one who acted as relief.

Near Mount Camino, south of Mount Cassino, I saw my brother-in-law—a doctor—who had been wounded after forty-one days without changing his clothes. He was hit by a mortar fragment. I haven't been wounded in battle but here is how this boy felt:

He was with the battalion aid station up on Mount Camino. This station consisted of little more than a lot of courage, and a canvas flap with a red cross on it.

The men in the forward zones used to cover the red cross with mud so that it couldn't be spotted, because the Germans—at least in Italy—sometimes deliberately hit a hospital. If they saw the red cross they might use it as a target because they knew that the command post was nearby and if they could box that area with artillery they could hit communications.

At any rate, my brother-in-law was at the front and late in the afternoon he and some comrades started to heat coffee over a little gasoline stove. A mortar shell dropped nearby, and they picked themselves up—and then a second, and a third. Every time they reached for the coffee another shell came.

My brother-in-law took refuge behind a rock with four other men, lying elbow to elbow and holding onto their helmets. He was in the middle. The shells kept coming and they counted them. He thinks it was the eighteenth or nineteenth which got them. The boy on his far left was killed outright, the one next to him on that side was fatally injured, my brother-in-law was wounded in the shoulder—and the two on his right were not hurt at all.

Another medical officer dressed the shoulder. A shell fragment is red-hot and therefore often sterile, and because of the heat penetrates the flesh very easily. My brother-in-law didn't feel the wound greatly and it didn't bother him as much as the fact that he was deaf. He had no way of knowing, although he was a doctor, that he was only temporarily deaf. He was quite deaf when he woke up in the morning after lying there all night in a state of mild shock.

All he could think about was not the wound in his shoulder, or the fact that he had to go down the mountainside almost five miles to get a jeep to a collection station, or even the permanence of his deafness—but he was worrying because he couldn't hear the sound of a shell. He never had realized how much he listened to the war, but suddenly being deaf was worse than the wound. To be thus deprived of his ears meant that he had to keep an eye on some soldier perhaps several yards ahead of him. When the soldier heard a shell coming and dropped for cover, the doctor hit the dirt too. The end of the story is that within a few days his hearing was almost 100 per cent.

At the front there was very little formality between officers and enlisted men. They ate together and of course there was absolutely no saluting. At the battalion aid station there might be one or two doctors, eight medical corpsmen and perhaps a half-dozen litter bearers. This was not behind the front but was part of the fighting line.

All the stretcher bearers were volunteers. I can't think of any more hazardous work, because they can't defend themselves. It may be hazardous to unscrew a pin on a bomb or a mine, or hazardous to do something similar for one afternoon, but these noble fellows serve day after day. If a soldier is shot and falls they go and get him. They are wonderful boys!

The blackout in the combat section right near the front lines was nearly 100 per cent so far as concerned cigarettes, flashlights and matches. Consequently, the putting of a tag on a wounded man who was being transported back was a problem. The stretcher bearers had to dig a hole, get a blanket under which they could use a light, or write in the dark.

Naturally most of the injuries occurred during the day, although the German artillery would open up and work at night if they knew precisely where the target was. This meant that most of the transportation was done during the day although the movement and treatment of the wounded was a twenty-four-hour-a-day job.

I studied anatomy as an art student, and my father is a doctor. I'm interested in medicine and know pretty well what the human body consists of, but I never realized there were so many bones in the body until I saw these wounded boys. We normally think of a bullet wound as being a hole in the fleshy part of the body, but what the bullets do to a bone is ghastly. I saw one soldier who had his lung ripped, three ribs fractured, his shoulder injured badly and the bone in his upper arm damaged with just one bullet.

over the typewriting. From then on until they were to go home there was a slow drop.

There were some horrible instances of eye injuries from frost-bite among members of our air corps based in England, where I also worked. At altitudes of 25,000 and 35,000 feet temperatures of 40 to 50 degrees below zero are "normal," and an eye may be lost by very brief exposure to the cold air. Fingers also become frost-bitten in 10 or 12 seconds if gloves are taken off. The fingers look almost like little blue bananas. It is very much like a badly burned hand and I think that medically frost-bite and burns are akin.

We have another fine example of improvisation in the case of the loss of eyes. That was in the development by two dentists of acrylic resin instead of glass for artificial eyes. The demand for artificial eyes was considerable and couldn't be met quantitatively because most of them came from Germany. The dentists made artificial eyes by baking the acrylic resin and painting it, and they could match it even to the flecks in the cornea.

(Surgeon General Kirk has said: "These acrylic eyes are fitted to the eye-socket in the same way that dentures are fitted to the mouth. Besides fitting perfectly, these new eyes are much lighter and less fragile than the old glass eye.")

(Artist Hirsch has mentioned one of the great hazards of the air—frost-bite—but there are many others which make aviation a definite field of medical specialization due, to quote Deputy Air Surgeon Charles R. Glenn, "to the inescapable fact that man in flight is a different animal from that earthbound creature with whom other specialists are accustomed to deal."

(The airman encounters many unusual death-dealing forces which are capable of injuring or killing him. Barometric pressure and temperature at high altitudes are among these. The flier has to learn, too, that if he is to survive he must maintain rigid oxygen discipline. An attempt to breathe free air between 20,000 and 30,000 feet would result in death in a few moments.

(Then, as General Glenn says, "each man has his flying efficiency curve and the best of them will reach a point in that curve where he will break down himself or crack up his plane. The breakdown common to combat fliers is called operational fatigue."

(The list of unusual dangers with which the flier has to contend is a long one. So while the medical problems of aviation ground-crews are much the same as those of the foot-soldier, the airman presents a very special case which the Medical Corps handles through experts in aviation medicine.)

The Medical Department can gauge our Army morale in any part of the world, and morale can't be uniform when it involves millions of men. In Italy, where I was, it wasn't too good. The doctors

Another great problem which the Medical Corps had to face was treatment of the blind. Fortunately very few boys were totally blinded, that is, lost the sight of both eyes. Many of them—thousands—lost one eye. In the case of the blind men the experts in the war zone wanted to teach the boys how to be blind so that when they came back to America they could walk down the gangplank with all the assurance that the sightless person ultimately acquires.

However, it didn't work out that way because after a few weeks of cooperation the injured man's nostalgia for America became overpowering. For that reason many of them were brought back for treatment in the hospital at Valley Forge, Pennsylvania, then for reconditioning at Old Farms Convalescent Hospital, Avon, Connecticut, before they were ready to take off their uniforms and proceed as successful blind people.

I was told that the rise and fall of the spirit of blinded boys was almost the same in every case. At first they were almost suicidal from very deep melancholy. One of the earliest things they were taught was how to typewrite—that is, after they had learned how to feed themselves and get to the bathroom. When they found that they were getting every attention and that all their wants were anticipated —that they could indeed find their way to the bathroom, feed themselves, and typewrite—their spirits rose and they became almost exhilarated, especially

all told me that the length of the line in front of the clinic at 8 A.M. was directly in proportion to the morale of the troops and to the nearness to the front. In a sector where morale wasn't good, a doctor in the rear echelon would report by eight o'clock and be finished by nine. Farther forward he might report at eight and not be finished until one.

Just what proportion in line were gold-bricking and just what proportion were afflicted with a cold —or whatever the complaint happened to be—is something I don't know. But there was very little gold-bricking in the rear echelon. And the doctors had a pretty accurate gauge of morale in the number of applicants who showed up at the hospital.

I am talking about non-combat patients. In a few instances—a very few—there were self-inflicted injuries, but a boy who inflicted an injury on himself was usually psychoneurotic to a degree. I remember seeing one who had shot himself in the foot, and the story, always the same, was: "I was cleaning my gun and it went off."

But the men who were genuinely hurt were very cooperative with the doctor whereas the others were evasive in their answers. One lad had taken his shoe off and then shot his foot and put the shoe back on again. In general, gold-bricking is a very reliable measure of morale.

Another thing: The men who pass through the hands of the Army doctors, after having been wounded in battle, are a different kind of animal than the soldiers who haven't suffered physically at the hands of the enemy. They have a more substantial realization of what the war is about. I remember in particular seeing the reaction of about 5,000 soldiers in a personnel replacement depot. That was where wounded boys went after recuperation—before being sent back to the United States, into limited service or back to combat again.

One night the men had assembled in the big grandstand of a horse-racing track where the replacement depot was located, and they were waiting for the sun to sink sufficiently so that the movies would be visible on the screen. During this wait there were some news flashes over the loudspeaker. One of the flashes from home was that the cost of the war to the United States up to that time had far exceeded one hundred billion dollars, but that America was ready to spend another billion dollars to speed victory.

You could hear a gasp of surprise and a wave of muttered exclamations of disgust and curses. These boys, who didn't think at all in terms of dollars, much less in terms of billions of dollars—who had lost completely any habit of thinking in such terms —suddenly heard this statement, which was so irrelevant to that vertebra that had been pulled out of place, or the bullet in the thigh or arm. To hear the war expressed in terms of dollars was a shock.

The very infliction of a wound in battle gives a man a different slant. Consequently I think the Medical Corps more than any separate department of the Army has a particularly advantageous position insofar as gauging the change that comes to veterans of combat. I met many boys who had been in four amphibious invasions, and one who had been in five, and up to a certain point they became battle-toughened veterans. After that point their efficiency —but more their spirit—definitely dropped.

The number of venereal patients treated by the Medical Corps was the biggest problem in certain areas—that is, statistically. In the South Pacific, malaria took precedence.

So far as medical prophylaxis for venereal disease was concerned, there certainly was no shortage. The doctors had to deal with the final results, but there was a whole prior chain of events. A kid was subjected to nervous strain and tension during battle, and on his leave he didn't deliberately decide to find a female and become infected with venereal disease—although on occasion it is a form of gold-bricking—but he simply got drunk and careless. I should say that about 95 per cent of the boys so infected were drunk. They were drunk and irresponsible, and they forgot.

On any reports having to do with a patient, whether discharged or otherwise, always was the clause: "In the line of duty—yes; In the line of duty—no." Of course if a boy got careless and was hospitalized with pneumonia, it was in the line of duty. But not so in the case of venereal disease.

There are two sides to this problem. On the one hand you have doctors invoking the Hippocratic oath that a patient is a patient and should be so treated. But on the other hand, a man of about 50 said to me in great heat:

"Hirsch, you are an artist. You want to get back and paint pictures. I want to get back to cardiology. Everybody wants to get back. And those who deliberately or accidentally become infected venereally, in spite of all the provisions that the Medical Corps

has to prevent infection, are absenting themselves from their jobs in the Army. They are occupying hospital beds where bad cases should be. They are prolonging the war."

(These two viewpoints of course raise the much debated question of whether fighting men who contract venereal disease should be punished. The method of dealing with this troublesome problem varies in different countries. Some inflict heavy penalties, especially where the disease is contracted through infraction of rules.)

In the army there is nothing backward about the preventive measures, although in many areas of America there are backward people. All over the war theatre there were signs: "Beware of V.D.," or "Caution—V.D.," or in some places "Venereal disease bad." The prophylaxis stations bore the sign "Pro Station."

Incidentally, a very funny thing happened in connection with these "pro station" signs. Shortly after we moved into Naples, the Army public relations office, where all the correspondents checked in —British and American—posted a sign outside. This was "PRO," meaning public relations office, but the initials weren't separated by periods. As a result it was several times confused for a "pro station" by bewildered GIs who ran into it.

In January of 1944, before the Allied Control Commission was set up in the Naples area, our Army Medical Corps had the responsibility of combating the seriously threatening epidemic of typhus. It was serious insofar as it contaminated the area and the civilians—even though none of our inoculated soldiers contracted the disease—for we used Italians to drive our jeeps and to do our work for us. Contamination of food and water supplies would be very dangerous. The Medical Corps did splendid work.

I went around with the lice-squad one night when we visited nine underground "recoveros" or air-raid shelters. Two or three of them were without doubt the filthiest places I ever have seen, including some of the slum areas in Spain and Shanghai. The shelters were damp and there were puddles of urine. My flashlight picked up squashed rats. It was in the air-raid shelters that the typhus epidemic spread, and we sent down men with DDT powder. By using that powder and a lot of elbow grease they held the line and won the battle. But it was serious in January of '44.

About six or seven miles outside Naples the Fascists had a World's Fair in 1940, and on the site of these fair grounds the United States Army set up a medical center. This consisted of five or six hospitals. One of my paintings shows an orthopedic ward—a couple of rows of beds with our banged-up boys, and back of them on the walls by the high ceilings were big Fascist photo murals of an Italian soldier and Mussolini's ideology in quotation. Bombardment by us and later by the Germans had cracked the walls. I thought the juxtaposition of the cracking walls and the broken bones in the boys being mended made a striking picture. On top of these murals—as another example of GI impudence and disdain—were pin-up girls. The incongruity was wonderful!

The diversity of the Medical Corps undertakings was amazing. I visited an evacuation hospital devoted entirely to the treatment of our Allies. I saw a seventy-year-old woman being cared for in an Army hospital.

A Corpsman carried a woman, who was about to have a baby, out of the path of a stream of lava from Vesuvius. Then, about twenty minutes before the lava came down, a corps doctor delivered her while the volcanic ashes dropped around them. This doctor also attended two sheep belonging to the woman.

So far as the psychoneurotic question is concerned, it is the biggest problem in relation to the knowledge which we have to combat it. We know a lot about broken bones, and about malaria, but not so much about psychoneurosis.

Many boys who were temporarily psychoneurotic would insist upon being sent back to the front and it wasn't very often that the doctors refused such a request. A general hospital was the only one which could send a soldier back to the United States.

One soldier arrived in Algiers from Naples on his way home—a psychoneurotic case—who apparently was the victim of a mistake on the part of the doctors in Naples, since he seemed to be normal. But one day while he was in hospital in Algiers an airplane zoomed low over the building in violation of regulations—and this so-called normal boy was found under his bed completely shaken.

When a soldier was sent home, it was for a very good reason. Many were assigned to permanent limited service.

Simulated psychoneurosis is really a form of the affliction. A man who is willing to be branded as a neurotic— as having cracked—is, to a degree, neurotic. If he is crazy enough to shoot himself in the leg, he has reached what they call his emotional threshold.

The problem of how long to keep men in combat is naturally a serious one. I questioned some German prisoners about this, at a compound where several hundred of them were being treated by their own doctors under American supervision. I asked two German doctors how to explain the absence of psychoneurosis cases in a hospital taking care of 700 prisoners.

Their explanation was that the German spartan environment—the early military training—was more re-enforcing than American football, basketball and tennis. My own explanation was that those Germans who were sufficiently close to us to be captured were healthy. I figured that they must have cases which were not in the front lines.

The German doctors did say that letters from home indicated there were a lot of psychoneurotic disturbances among the civilians. Somehow I didn't think that was a shame.

Injured fliers transported by dog sled.

6

D-Day in Normandy

THE United States Army Medical Corps won a Purple Heart on the historic D-Day of June 6, 1944 —for the Corpsmen swarmed up onto the shell-swept, bloody beaches of Normandy with the first three waves of Allied fighting men.

This greatest of all amphibious invasions was much as the experts had dreamed it would be. An Allied armada of 4,000 ships drove across a stormy English Channel towards the five landing beaches which had been selected. There had been a heavy air bombardment the night before, and as the fleet moved in with the coming of the dawn every gun went into action. Cruisers and destroyers rammed their noses right up to the shore, and some even struck bottom.

Our greatest losses at the outset were on the heavily mined beaches which were under a vicious enemy cross-fire. Because of these mines we couldn't bury the dead until D+3, as the engineers were so busy clearing out mines for the forces that the graveyards had to wait.

The Corpsmen were among the earliest arrivals on the beach-heads and their losses were heavy. The medical men had their little stations along the sands and were not only under shell-fire but were sniped continually by the Germans. Surgeons performed major operations on these beach-heads.

All the members of the corps had been specially trained in England for this great emergency, and they did a grand job. Many of them didn't sleep for 48 hours, for the wounds were bad in those first few days.

Medical supplies kept coming from Britain in the narrow water lanes which Allied vessels had swept through the German mine fields. The landing boats which took troops to the beach-heads brought wounded back to the ships. Some of these landing craft were specially fitted so that stretchers could be put on them in tiers.

Into this unprecedented scene, fortune flung Artist Lawrence Beall Smith, who risked his life to gather the story which he now presents:

In England when they were getting set for D-Day there was a terrific sense of the impending event— of the probabilities that there would be awful casualties. Preparations never before envisaged were made to meet the anticipated casualties.

During the last week the tension was almost unbearable. You couldn't help but know that things were moving. Many war correspondents and photographers had left London and were on their way. It was very reasonable to assume that things were pretty close.

There was a stepping up of air activity. Every morning the noise of the bombers going over seemed to be greater. If you went down into what they called the "restricted area" near the coast it was obvious that things were ready. From the looks of the place they couldn't find much more room for men and supplies. The troops had been waiting without leave for two and a half months. It couldn't last much longer.

On the morning of D-Day it was obvious that the great moment had arrived, because the roar of the warplanes overhead was incredible. There were hundreds of them in the air at once. You could feel the released tension in London after it was announced that the invasion was under way.

But to start at the beginning, I left New York in February and made my headquarters in London. The first material I went after was air corps medicine, and my point of departure was the American Eighth Air Force Headquarters. The Eighth was flying B-17's and this created a big medical problem, since these were ten-man planes.

I got to see the constant operation in connection with what, at that time, was an enormous offensive. There was a vast difference between air corps medicine and ground medicine. For instance, they were having a lot of trouble with frost-bite. Gunners got their fingers frozen from the cold air coming through the vents by their guns. Sometimes the face or eyes would be badly frozen. The nose of the ship might be sawed off and allow an inrush of destructive frigid air. If men forgot to put on their gloves in bailing out, their hands would freeze. Frost-bite sometimes caused gangrene. This could be checked but the treatment was slow and laborious.

The whole set-up for medical treatment in connection with the air corps warfare was well stabilized. Each one of the air bases would have several station hospitals within a few miles, so that the men who did come back wounded could be transported easily to a well-equipped hospital.

They had many rest homes which were not convalescent places but establishments to which they could send those men who were on the verge of a nervous breakdown or who needed simple release from tension. The strain in the air war is complete unto itself so far as the business of bombers is concerned. These men fly through flak over a target. They know that sooner or later they are bound to get hit. It's just a case of sweating out their series of missions and trusting to luck. There is very little maneuvering they can do.

Unlike the infantrymen who live in miserable surroundings all the time, day and night in mud and cold, these fliers go off on their missions at dawn—long missions may take ten hours—and when they return to base they get a shower, fresh clothes, and go to an officers' club. There they have a pleasant bar where they get plenty to drink and to eat. Then they go away at dawn the next morning.

Their day is divided into terrific danger and almost complete normalcy. This causes the tension which results in breakdowns, as does the steady diet of the infantry. It is a particular kind of tension that the infantry doesn't understand.

The rest homes were instituted with the idea that they would give just as little suggestion of war as was possible. At these rest homes the men got out of uniform. They broke all routine and they slept throughout the day if they wanted to do so. This made a complete change. Some airmen reacted violently the first couple of days. They wanted to finish their missions. After that, however, they were all right. They had every conceivable kind of thing to keep them entertained.

D-Day found me in the throes of credential difficulties, which I finally solved on June 11. After the first night of the V-1 bomb I left the next day for southern England to witness the return of early casualties.

I watched this constant procession of the wounded as they came from the beach-heads. They were brought back on enormous LSTs and then were transferred to smaller LCTs which went into the English beaches. By the time the LSTs came back they were the most miserable sights I ever have seen. The weather couldn't have been worse. The problem with the LSTs was the fact that it was a 14-hour trip from the time they started, and then there was another five or six hours waiting for tides, and sometimes air raids or storms held them up.

There were occasions when the casualties were packed on the tank decks for two or three days because of such complications. Another difficulty from the medical standpoint was that the wounded had to be handled so often during this transporting. The Corpsmen would put them on one ship, transfer them to another, and then carry them to ambulances. That was three handlings. Many of them were severe litter cases and each move meant a strain.

Among the thousands of wounded whom I saw returning from Normandy, I seldom heard a groan out of anybody. A huge transport would be full of wounded men, many of them in agony, but rarely would you hear a moan or a complaint. I think it was mostly a matter of mass feeling. If one man had opened up, ten others would have told him to shut up. The wounded didn't often ask attention of any man. They just accepted their particular fate.

At Portland they built special docks for the LSTs. While they were unloading wounded men from one ship they were loading another nearby with fresh troops and tanks. It was psychologically bad and the confusion was terrible. The atmosphere was tense.

The transportation problem alone was staggering. Just as far as the eye could see there was that endless, steady stream of vehicles. The unloading of an LST was a slow, laborious job. Negro litter bearers would take off the casualties one by one until the smaller ships were filled.

They had two Navy doctors attached to the LST and after the heavy rush began they added an Army doctor. With them were non-professional Corpsmen and anyone else who could help. The wounded ran to over 400 on one of these ships. The walking wounded were on the top deck, weather permitting.

One of the enormous problems for the artist was the fact that this whole operation was so vast that it almost staggered you to know where to begin. You saw thousands of casualties. You saw thousands of ships—wounded men coming in and fresh troops and supplies pouring out. There was material to use everywhere and always the knowledge that you wouldn't have time to do it all. It was just a question of trying to pick out characteristic things which hit you as pictorial.

After about five days there I hopped an LST and took a trip across to Normandy. I went in on what was known as Omaha Beach. I arrived right after the big storm and it looked as though another invasion had taken place. It was a terrific mess. Small ships were crashed up on the beach and there were a few sunken craft in front of it. Many of the placements and piers, which the seabees and engineers had built, were askew or completely destroyed.

We carried over a complete set of tanks on the tank-deck, and after we had run our huge ship up on the beach I watched the whole procession of tanks roar down to the shore. It wasn't more than half an hour after they departed, and the odor of carbon monoxide was still in the air, when they started to bring in the casualties. Litters were placed on the ship where the treads of the tank tires still showed—these monstrous tanks going out first and then the miserable litter cases coming in. All this was during a blackout with intermittent enemy planes overhead, which emphasized the macabre feature of the thing.

All the men attached to the Medical Corps were working very hard, right around the clock. Carrying litters, for instance, is a tough job. They are heavy. The litter men were under the constant strain of going up inclines without shaking the patients. They really worked like dogs to fill a whole ship with casualties.

I hitched a ride with one of the ambulances which had brought wounded men to our ship. It was as black as ink. You couldn't see a thing. I rode on this ambulance to the original D-Day clearing station which was right on the beach-head behind the air strip. The fighting was very heavy in the direction of St. Lô.

I went to the field hospital attached to the 29th Division in the St. Lô sector. I spent the rest of my time in Normandy with that division and with the 30th, alternating between the two as the fighting shifted. I made my headquarters at the field hospital, going up into the forward areas during the day.

The first medical unit was the battalion aid station which was connected with the infantry and was usually a hundred yards behind the line. Generally a few hundred yards behind the aid station was a collecting company. The transportation of the wounded between these two was done by jeep, which was a big advance over the last war. These jeeps would carry three or four litter cases. At the collecting station the wounded might be given a little more treatment. Then they were put into ambulances and were rushed back to a clearing station.

The clearing station was a clearing point for all types of wounded, from the man who had a scratch on one of his fingers to the chap with a severe abdominal wound. The men who were badly hurt were not transported back any farther but were sent across to the field hospital, which was attached to the clearing station.

Only grave cases, however, went across to the field hospital from the clearing station—cases in which men were in danger of dying if they were moved any farther back from the front. The other wounded were sent to evacuation hospitals in the rear.

The field hospital was the farthest forward that surgery went. They tried to keep the field hospital four to six miles back from the fighting zone. They figured that four miles was the closest point at which they still could have a degree of safety from artillery.

Because of the closeness of the field hospitals to the front, almost invariably they were set up near units of our own artillery. That was a deafening place for men who were so sick, especially when our guns started barrages. Then the ground literally shook. Gunfire would do anything but quiet the nerves of men in that condition. All of them had suffered shock and had to be brought out of it before they could be operated upon.

When one of the big barrages opened up, it started about 5:30 in the morning and went on for perhaps two solid hours. The gun batteries were on both sides of the field hospitals. It sounded as though they were automatics.

At the clearing station there was a place where they had battle exhaustion cases. During one of the barrages some of these men went completely haywire and tried to dig fox-holes in the ground with their hands. They had to be rounded up like sheep.

This was going on in all of the tents in a less obvious way. Most of the wounded felt the same although they were too sick to move. Every one of these chaps in the field hospital was a very sick man or he would have been sent farther back out of the noise.

Most of the treatment of battle exhaustion was by giving sleeping pills. The men slept their exhaustion off and were sent right back into the lines. These particular men who "blew their tops" had just moved in that afternoon and had not yet been treated. Most of these exhaustion cases snapped out of it. A few did not.

At that time whole-blood was being supplied by Britain. Whole-blood is much more beneficial than plasma. Shock breaks a man's blood down and this will kill him in a very short time unless his blood is replaced. The blood content of the body is great and a wounded man has to have a lot given him before he comes out from shock.

So pint after pint of whole-blood was used and at one point the outfit I was with ran out of it. There were two shock tents, containing thirty men each, and they could only be brought out of shock by pouring blood into them. The doctors got about eight volunteers from the exhaustion tent. These weary men gave their blood. They volunteered although they appeared to be out on their feet. It was an impressive sight.

The shock tents were terribly quiet places. They had a certain atmosphere about them—a kind of tension—that was depressing. There was little raving. The men lay very still and breathed hard. There was the feeling in many instances that it was a borderline case. Would the blood do it, or would it not?

The combat at this time was mainly a battle of hedgerows. The Americans would gain a hedgerow across a field and the Germans would counterattack. Most of the fighting seemed to be with artillery, mortars and mines, all of which caused terrible wounds. It was seldom during the time I was there that I saw a really clean bullet wound. The men had multiple wounds.

During pushes the Army Medical Corps surgical teams worked 16-hour shifts. They had auxiliary surgical units which would move from one platoon to another. All field hospitals had three platoons and when one platoon would get heavy casualties, an auxiliary would go up and help out.

The auxiliary team generally was composed of a commanding officer—usually a major—three surgeons, an anesthetist and four enlisted handy-men, who worked in many capacities and took the place of nurses. One of these units had been through the Salerno and Anzio landings and this was its third invasion.

They had nurses at the field hospitals. It was a rough life for a woman. They didn't go any farther forward at that time than the field hospital. It was a tough spot and a very uncomfortable existence. In the first place they were moving all the time. As the front would advance they would pack up and follow on. The speed of the movement made it difficult.

There was intermittent German air activity at night. The danger was mostly from our own flak, which was sent up and had to come down. Most of the nurses looked weary, but they did a wonderful job and the fact that they were there helped a great deal. The psychological effect was very good. At least one nurse worked in the shock tent all the time.

Sometimes it was necessary to dig fox-holes for protection against bombing. However, as the battle progressed there wasn't as much enemy air activity as had been expected. The fox-holes were dug with a little less enthusiasm than at first.

The Germans didn't use any flying bombs in Normandy while I was there. These were miserable things. The robots which came over the area seemed to be on their way somewhere else. Seldom did anything drop. But our flak was sent up, and it fell down on the tents.

The operating rooms were all blacked-out. The tents were fool-proof so far as light was concerned, having been specially constructed. At the entrance they put double doors and two curtains. Most of the surgical tents that I saw had an inner lining of white. They found that the light reflected off this white sheeting.

The lighting was done with portable dynamos and was just adequate, but it was all they could get with the power they had. They had accessory lighting which would show up the specific feature of an operation. During the rush period I often helped by holding a little handlight that was made with a couple of tins which had held blood plasma. This spotlight was devised by an enlisted Corpsman.

One of the surgeons was a chest specialist, and I watched him frequently. I became fascinated by the whole business. I saw hundreds of operations of all kinds and occasionally found myself doing things which I never had thought that I could do. At one time I held a leg that was being amputated. Thus much of the material in surgery appealed to me clinically greatly, but pictorially was far behind other subjects which I chose.

The doctors and enlisted Corpsmen were quick to meet emergencies and improvise. They were forced to do this by the conditions under which they lived. The surgical teams I was with hit the beachhead about D + 1. One of these teams hung there on Omaha Beach, just hoping they could live to do something. All that could be done at that time was temporary first aid. They didn't set up surgery for some time after that.

The surgeons in the majority of the groups that I observed were from 35 to 46 years old. I saw two men at the field hospital who must have been in their fifties. It was a rough life for a man of that age, to say nothing of the 16-hour shift strain.

The surgical specialists, of course, had to pitch in. They might have a dozen chest cases alone. They sometimes performed two and three major operations on one man, and they didn't know how these boys lived through it. I saw one case where two surgeons worked on the same man. He had an arm amputated and then had a stomach operation. They turned him over and found the whole fleshy part of one of his legs gone. They were afraid of gangrene and so they cut away a great deal of tissue. All three of these things were done under the same anesthesia. Four days later this boy was better off than some of the others.

Sometimes there were double amputations. One amputation is a terrific shock. They did everything they could to save a limb. In cases of bad wounds they would try to fix the main artery and would go to immense pains to avoid amputation. They always had consultations on all amputations.

35

The wounded were moved from the field hospital at the earliest possible time. Since the field hospital was constantly filling up, the men had to be evacuated. They were so sick that their post-operative care was an enormous problem. When a field hospital moved forward, it very often was necessary to leave post-operative cases behind under the care of one of the doctors.

The minute a man could be moved he was sent to the evacuation hospital. There he might be operated on for a second time or have a new cast put on a fracture. The evacuation hospital was a well-equipped and fairly stable unit, and the general hospital was even more so. They were tent hospitals, but huge, and had many nurses and doctors. The surgical tent would have 15 operations going on all at once. The first general hospital arrived in Normandy early in July. Most of the cases were going from the evacuation hospitals by air or by ships to general hospitals in England.

The Army Medical Corps had many unusual situations to meet. I remember that once when I was in England one of our bombers crashed and blew up, and 10 of the men were killed. It was the first mission for all of them. The force of the explosion boosted me out of bed at the base, a mile and a half away. The Medical Corps had to take care of these casualties, as there was no one else to do it. It was a question of salvaging as much as they could. They got the equivalent of six bodies out of the wreckage. (This is Smith's picture "Death of a B-17.")

I was with a collecting company unit which set up at a village outside of St. Lô. This was about 800 yards back of the fighting line and the village was in flames. The unit had one tent and they put it up in the churchyard. They hadn't been there for more than half the day when the Germans began pouring shells all around this area, and the unit suffered two casualties. The Corpsmen moved to a safe spot and then 24 hours later came back to the same place and re-established themselves. (This scene is depicted in Smith's "Sunday in Normandy.")

When this unit set up in the cemetery the men started to dig their fox-holes right away. The fox-holes looked like graves, and the fellows scattered all over digging these holes appeared rather ghoulish. Incidentally, it was extremely interesting to see how many churches stood up under fire. They must have been pretty well built.

(There perhaps was a further reason why these churches survived. During the last war the writer saw numerous instances in France where churches were left standing because gunners and bombers deliberately avoided hitting them.

(There was, for example, the case of the Golden Virgin which stood atop the church in the town of Albert, on the Somme. This was a heroic size figure of the Virgin, holding the Christ Child, and you could see it for miles across the valley when the sun glinted off the gilt. Both Allied and German fighting men did their best to avoid damage to this statue, and the tradition grew up that the side which destroyed the Golden Virgin would lose the war. Finally one day a German gunner shot down the statue—and sure enough, the Reich was defeated.)

The aid men to me were an extremely heroic lot. I tried in one picture to show a typical aid man. All were haggard, and very tired. They seemed like young old men; they had a kind of haunted look. They were the first medical help that the wounded man got. They were under fire just as much as the infantry. They didn't carry arms and were absolutely non-combatant. Their only protection was the red cross.

The red cross was plastered all over them. Only seldom was the red cross not respected by the Germans. One surgical team, which went in with the gliders on D-Day, set up in an open field. They had a big tarpaulin with a red cross on it, and they were left unmolested.

(The reader should note that Artist Smith is speaking of Normandy. There were instances in other European theatres in which the Germans did not respect the red cross.)

These battalion aid men were on the firing line with the troops. They rushed to the wounded men who had fallen, gave them morphine and any other emergency treatment feasible. The aid men carried a fair amount of equipment and could give plasma or bandage a wound. The injured man was provided as much shelter as possible, had a tag put on him and ordinarily was left for the litter bearers to pick up and take to the battalion aid station. Sometimes the aid man himself would carry back the wounded soldier.

There was no tent for the battalion aid station. It was located in any likely spot—under a tree or a hedgerow. There was a doctor and he had enough equipment to give temporary first aid. He didn't attempt surgery, for the most part.

However, they got the man on a litter or jeep back to the collecting station in a few minutes. The speed of evacuation was remarkable. Within an hour or two a man would be moved to a field hospital from the point at which he fell on the battlefield. The efficiency struck me as being extraordinary.

The aid men used to come back a few hundred yards from the front to a collecting station, for the purpose of rest and quiet. The station was like a grand hotel to them. These boys would be sleeping in the fox-holes at the collecting station when they would be awakened and told that it was time to go up to the battalion aid station. They would hop on a jeep and off they would go to the front again.

My reaction was that the Corpsmen get into the spirit of the thing just as the doctors do. They feel like men who are treating sick people rather than like GIs assigned to duty at a given point.

So far as the surgeons and other medical men were concerned it was a chance for them to do professional work and experimentation. They handled cases they never would get in civilian life—cases that perhaps they never would see again.

They did fantastic feats of surgery but they rarely could follow their cases through. They didn't learn whether the men upon whom they had operated had survived. Most of the surgeons didn't try to check up on their cases.

Apropos of this, before going to Normandy I had encountered in England the case of a German prisoner who had been operated on in the fighting zone. The doctors in Britain couldn't understand why the operation had been performed in a certain unusual way. After I got to Normandy I happened to mention this case to one of our doctors, and he recalled that he had performed the operation. He had a good reason for doing it as he did, and was delighted to hear how it turned out.

Speaking of German prisoners, enemy wounded were treated in the same way as our own men, with the exception that the Americans always were given priority. For instance, on LSTs all German walking wounded were the last off the ship and were the last in line at the hospitals.

There was a definite feeling of tension between American paratroopers and German prisoner wounded on the LSTs. The first day I was on an LST I went down into the tank deck and it took me a half hour to get my equilibrium. I had just been reading Tolstoy's "War and Peace," and the stench and the atmosphere on the tank deck were exactly as in the hospital scene described by the book.

A wounded man motioned to me and pointed to the blanket which had fallen off his injured leg. I put the blanket back, and an American soldier lying nearby called to me:

"I'll bet there is no other place in the world where that thing could happen."

It was a German prisoner for whom I had rearranged the blanket. I hadn't known that at the time.

When my work in Normandy was done I flew back to London and prepared for the return home. I came back to the States on a hospital ship which was making its maiden voyage, and the continued treatment of the wounded men on the vessel was interesting.

There were about 500 patients on the ship all told. Some appeared to be hopeless cases. Then there were a lot of very bad cases which were out of danger so far as death was concerned although they had a long hill ahead of them. These were sent back to the States as soon as possible.

The ship was a floating palace, and it had wonderful medical equipment. The wards were congested because all available places were filled with beds, and there were many double-decker bunks. They brought across mental cases and there was a special place for them.

It was a beautiful set-up. The food was excellent, and the men who were able to get out could enjoy the sun and had a good rest.

7

Burma Road

FEW THEATRES of war held so much human interest as Burma, due partly to the mystery surrounding this primeval region which pokes its head up into China and Tibet right under the "roof of the world," and partly to the fact that over a long and dangerous period for the Allies it was the lifeline of hard-hit China to outside countries.

Few theatres, too, produced such abnormal and onerous military problems. Great names fill the history of the Allied campaign which finally evicted the Japanese from this strategic territory—Stilwell, Merrill and his Marauders, Chennault, Wingate and his Raiders, and others. All these dared mightily in the Burmese jungle and in the adjacent fields of towering Chinese mountains to smash the Mikado's men and re-open the famous Burma Road.

The most difficult part of this warfare in the wilds wasn't the fight against the Japanese, but against Mother Nature herself who used this ageless zone as a laboratory for strange and awful experiments. There in the dense jungle the warring forces fought fierce heat and humidity, diseases that killed, and terrible forms of death from crawling things.

Into this wilderness went the United States Army Medical Corps, to play a vital part in the Allied victory. The task of recording the corps' activities on canvas was assigned to Howard Baer, whose pictures in this book afford an accounting of his stewardship. As in the case of our other artists, I passed long hours with Baer, listening to the story of his experiences—an account in which I was doubly interested because I knew India, the Burma Road, and China at first-hand. Here is what he told me:

I flew into the jungle from India in a hospital plane at the beginning of May, 1944, and landed about 50 miles from the headquarters of General Stilwell (General Joseph W. Stilwell, commander of the Chino-American forces in Burma, who was affectionately known as "Uncle Joe"). He was at Shadazup, southeast of Ledo, and I had to proceed from the airfield by jeep.

(At this time Stilwell's armies and engineers were extending the Ledo Road southeastwards from the Indian province of Assam toward Myitkyina in order to make a junction with the Burma Road. There was bloody fighting, for the Japanese were in force in that part of northern Burma.)

It was the monsoon season with its heavy rains, and the field we landed on was just a soupy mass. It was very difficult to get the planes up, and sometimes they couldn't land at all because it had rained so much for several days. Clay is the basic substance in that region, and as we went along the road there would be ruts so big that the jeep would be hung up. That was the normal condition of the terrain.

Stilwell's headquarters was on the Ledo Road, around which the jungle formed a solid wall. A man could be 15 paces away and you wouldn't see him. Every morning you were awakened about five o'clock by the weird chattering of monkeys. You never could see them, but they were on all sides. There were many sorts of flowers and strange plants. Trailing vines crept everywhere.

On and off the rains were a deluge, and sometimes there were terrible winds like hurricanes, so strong that they would rip limbs off trees. The temperature was hot and sticky—running from 110° to 120° F. You couldn't tell where the sweat ended and the rain began, and so I often left my raincoat off. We slept in jungle hammocks that had mosquito-net sides. They were shaped like a coffin. The wounded were on cots under nets.

The new road was being built while we fought the Japs. They were all around us—always infiltrating —always sniping. They also bombed the medical camps, but the jungle provided a natural camouflage.

The American Medical Corps was divided into platoons, and each platoon was located in a different section. The corps looked after Stilwell's picked Chinese troops, our American fighting engineers and Merrill's Marauders which comprised the U. S. forces in Burma.

I was with the medical platoon which was closest to the front. It was one of the portable surgical outfits which were the first to give a wounded man operative treatment. Before that he got quick bandaging at the first-aid station. Ambulances would go from the portable hospital to the first-aid station from which Chinese stretcher-bearers worked out into the firing zone. Our portable outfit, which was about three miles from the fighting front, was in little tents like a circus.

The majority of the doctors were young—in their twenties. It was a great experience for them because they were experimenting in many ways. They were terrifically energetic and worked all the time. Even the dentists were doing operations on other parts of the body. As a result every doctor got vast experience in operating.

The Cochins—aborigines who were head-hunters before the war—helped to carry in the wounded and also fought the Japs. These natives were brought into our service in a peculiar way. The jungle is filled with huge leeches—some several inches long—which drop from the trees and fasten themselves on human beings. If they are pulled off they may cause terrible sores. The best way to get them off is with salt or with a lighted match. Well, the Cochins were filled with sores from these leeches. Our medics cured them, and as a result the Cochins were so grateful that they offered their help. They were of great assistance to our troops in the jungle.

Our platoon had tents with open sides. There was also a basha—a little hut of bamboo poles with open sides and planks for tables. The whole outfit could be torn down and put on the road for moving to a new position within two hours. We went forward in trucks. Including surgeons and GIs there were about 50 men involved.

The hospital tent was divided into two. One was the reception part, to which the patients were brought in ambulances. There the wounded men were given morphine and a tetanus injection, and after that came plasma. Up to this point the patient had been given sulfa and had been bandaged out at the front. In the other part of the hospital tent was the operating theatre. Each outfit had a generator which gave the power for lighting. During an air-raid the current was turned off and all lights went out. Then masked flashlights were used until the surgeons had finished their work.

There was no end to the care that the surgeons gave the wounded men. I saw doctors probe for hours after a shell fragment. Finally they would take out a piece no bigger than a fingernail.

There were no American women nurses in the immediate vicinity of the front. The nurses who were in the jungle were back near Ledo at a place called Shinbyang, where there was an evacuation hospital carved out of the jungle. An evacuation hospital is a sort of advance base hospital, and this one was very efficient.

The nurses who were closest to the fighting were those who came in aboard the hospital planes. Whenever an airfield was captured, as at Myitkyina, the hospital planes would land and pick up the wounded. At that particular place Japanese planes came over and strafed our hospital planes.

The nurses really were very brave and they did an excellent job. They would fly with wounded men who had typhus, malaria, and other terrible diseases that one can contract in the jungle. There were all sorts of skin infections to be dealt with, and sores produced by the leeches and ticks. The nurses handled these men just like babies.

Each hospital plane carried a surgeon and two nurses, all members of the U. S. Army Medical Department. The plane had six tiers of brackets upon which stretchers were placed, and about 20 wounded men could be carried.

The evacuation nurses were former air stewardesses. All of them were very attractive, having been selected for their civilian jobs not only for ability but for appearance. These dainty little girls would handle the Indians, Chinese, British, Australians, Americans—a regular hodge-podge of troops—with equal care.

All these nationalities came into our hospitals. When they got farther back, there were British hospitals to take care of them. In the North Burma jungle they all went through the American Medical Corps. When our corps had done its work the patients were transferred to base hospitals in India.

The hospital planes took the wounded straight back to India. There were cases when a man who had been wounded near a landing field was in base hospital within four hours of the time he was injured.

The Chinese stretcher-bearers put the wounded in ambulances and brought them to the portable surgical unit where the American Medical Corps took complete charge. There the doctors would give emergency operations and put on plaster bandages to immobilize the tissue for evacuation to the rear, if the man was in condition to be flown back. If he wasn't able to travel he was kept at the station until he could be moved.

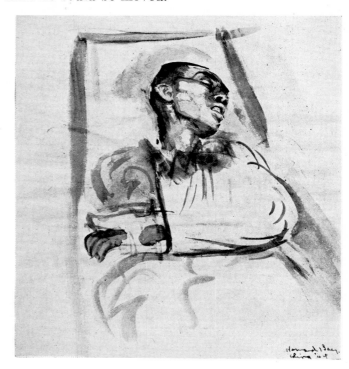

Myitkyina airfield was captured in a surprise attack by Merrill's Marauders and Chinese troops. (The exploits of our General Frank D. Merrill's special jungle contingent form a sensational chapter in the history of the fight for Burma.) For a time this airfield was the only section that the Marauders held at Myitkyina and they couldn't go off the field because the Japs were all around them. They had to clear the Japs out first.

Right after the capture of this airfield I came across the famous Colonel Seagrave, the man who wrote "Burma Surgeon," operating in a tent. (Artist Baer refers to Lt. Colonel Gordon S. Seagrave, an American medical missionary, who had practiced medicine and surgery on the Chinese border of Burma for some 20 years. In 1942 he joined the United States Army Medical Corps under Stilwell.)

There were litters holding wounded Chinese around Colonel Seagrave's tent. As I stood there, one wounded man fell over dead. The patient on the table was dying. The surgeon assisting Seagrave was pressing on the ribs of the dying man, attempting to revive him. The Colonel had his hand down the injured fellow's throat, trying to catch his tongue which he was swallowing.

There was another operation going on in the same tent. The Burmese nurses were moving about with instruments and were handing them to the surgeons as they were called for. A very short distance from the tent a Chinese 75 mm. gun was going off every half minute. Overhead our planes were circling and diving—bombing and strafing the Japanese gun emplacements which were within a quarter of a mile of the field. There were enemy snipers all around the field.

The Japanese planes would not attack while our warplanes were overhead. However, our fliers couldn't land because there were no facilities for refueling and so they had to fly back to their bases. As soon as they went away the Japanese bombers came over from airfields within 10 or 15 miles of the one we had captured.

The Japanese bombed Seagrave's tent, which bore no red cross. He went right on operating during the bombing and strafing. Seagrave is a powerfully built man, with a shock of gray hair. He has a booming voice and would yell for the instruments which he wanted. He was naked to the waist. He had a mask on at times.

Colonel Seagrave worked under constant high tension. He was steady, however, paying no attention to the war that was going on about him. He labored day and night. This description, by the way, applied equally to all the surgeons of the U. S. Army Medical Corps. They were magnificent.

There were many other surgeons in Burma who likewise were doing splendid work, but it happened that Seagrave was the one picked to operate at the Myitkyina post. The surgeons with him were young Americans who were getting the experience of their lives.

Colonel Seagrave had his own portable surgical unit, with about six surgeons and the attending GIs. He also had about ten Burmese nurses with him. They set up their operating place right on the airfield. The only protection they had against the monsoon weather was parachutes which had been used to drop supplies from our airplanes. These 'chutes were red, yellow, green, and blue—each color designating the type of supply which was being dropped. Seagrave set these parachutes up as tents.

There was no attempt at camouflaging them. The Japs knew we were there. At a distance of 15 yards the whole set-up looked like a very gay carnival. Yet underneath the parachutes there were dead and dying Chinese troops and Marauders. Colonel Seagrave and his surgeons were operating. Each group of people took on the color of the parachute under which they happened to be, as the rain would give way and the sun would strike down through the silk.

I noted a group of Chinese with many kinds of wounds under a yellow parachute. All of them, including some dead, were colored by the yellow silk. It was a horrible and fascinating effect—entirely unexpected and an anomaly in warfare.

This lasted only a couple of days, however, until we cleared the Japs away from that area. Then Seagrave dispensed with the colored parachutes and used huts. All of this happened during the monsoon deluge, with bursts of sun in between. Incidentally, the mosquitoes are bad during this season and Seagrave's outfit had no mosquito nets to protect them on the airfield, as the supply had run out.

The strain on the surgeons in that sector was terrific. They were operating in cramped conditions—under the constant threat of Jap patrols which were popping up through the jungle everywhere—under the threat of mosquitoes, bugs, heat and rain—under threat of dysentery, malaria, and scrub typhus (the reader will remember Artist Boggs' graphic description of this terrible form of typhus in the Southwest Pacific).

All this cut the men down, and they lost weight. There was atabrine on the dinner table for them, to ward off malaria. Some of them refused to take this medicine because it turned the skin yellow.

The members of the corps got taut and nervous, and if this had gone on long enough it is quite conceivable that they would have cracked up. But they stood up under it well.

The work they were doing was their life work. The experience in surgery was fascinating. They were young men and had an incentive for constant hard toil. They were very enthusiastic about it all. One surgeon would say to another:

"I'm getting tired of doing legs. Why don't you take legs and I'll take chests?"

They also had post-mortem exploratory experience, examining the havoc that a piece of shell can cause in the body.

I painted and sketched operations. I never had seen an operation before. Usually I can sketch very rapidly but when the surgeons were at work I found it very difficult at first to follow the operation, not knowing what was going on. Then, too, there was the smell of ether, and it was very hard to get used to the sight of the wounds. In each case they would put a bit into the man's mouth—a clasp that would prevent him from swallowing his tongue during the operation. There was a perforation in this clasp and the breath would come through it in a low, whistling sound. It was eerie.

The surgeons were very cooperative and they would explain things as they went along. I sketched with fountain pen on typewriter bond-paper. I did have watercolor paper but I very soon discovered that the moisture from the rains wouldn't leave the heavy paper, so I had to use the thinner bond. After sketching with a fountain pen I immediately would slap in water-color so that I would have a more complete sketch for development when I got home.

The dampness was so persistent that most of my sketches stayed moist until I eventually got hold of a 105 mm. shell-tube—a fiber tube with metal ends which holds the shell—and I rolled my sketches up and kept them in that, along with rice. The rice absorbed the moisture and kept my work dry.

While I was at the front there were a number of air raids. We had shell holes and dugouts to dive into when the enemy planes came over.

I drove up to the aid station by the firing line in a jeep with an executive officer. We could hear rifle fire getting louder as we went through the jungle. It was a nerve-shattering experience.

There was a solid wall of jungle on either side. You never knew when you might run into a Japanese patrol. The driver of the jeep got frightened and wouldn't go any farther, so we had to get out and walk the rest of the way. There were fox-holes spaced every 25 yards or so up the road, and as we walked along we kept our eyes on the next fox-hole so that we could dive into it for protection.

There also was danger to us at night from the Chinese sentries who were likely to shoot quickly if they heard a stranger coming. They would scream a challenge, and at the same time you would hear the click of their rifles. You had to act fast. You turned your flashlight up into your face so that the sentry could see you, and yelled like hell:

"Ding-how!!"

"Ding-how" is a broad Chinese term meaning "very good" or "everything is fine." The Chinese use it for all sorts of occasions, even in begging rides, when they stick up their thumbs, smile, and call out "ding-how."

But to get back to the Medical Corps operations, surgical teams consisting of approximately two surgeons with male nurses, and carrying their medical kits with them, would go up on the flanks behind the Japanese lines with Merrill's Marauders and do emergency operations. The Marauders moved on foot, traveling light and fast and making surprise attacks. The surgery was done under very primitive conditions. Only a local anesthetic was administered.

This is where the Piper Cub plane comes in. As soon as word was radioed out that there were wounded, Piper Cubs were flown in and landed in clearings in the jungle. These little planes evacuated one wounded man at a time, but in this way many lives were saved.

The surgical teams were under combat all the time. Merrill's Marauders were made up of the toughest, hand-picked men who were told when they volunteered that they would be on the move constantly in the jungle. They were from every walk of life.

The surgeons operated on a ground sheet. The operations were more or less crude, the patient gritting his teeth and taking it. The fortitude of the injured men was amazing. For example, there was the case of an American tank-man with the Chinese forces. He was gravely burned from head to toe when his tank got a direct hit. He tramped two and a half miles back through the Japanese lines to the aid station, and then was brought to the portable surgical station where he was bandaged all over. (See Baer's picture "Tank Casualty.")

CHINA

After some weeks in Burma I flew into China over "The Hump"—the famous pinnacle of the lofty mountain range in that region. The fighting then was along the Salween River, not far from the northeastern Burmese frontier.

The medical set-up in China was different. There were Chinese units which worked side by side with the American units. American portable surgical outfits with the Chinese troops were called medical pack trains. These comprised some two-score surgeons and Corpsmen who would move up over the precipices in the very rugged terrain across the Salween, with the aid of 15 to 20 Chinese horses which were built about like Shetland ponies. The Japanese held the Burma Road in that zone, so the Americans had to go through the mountains, and the trails were terribly difficult.

Each American medical unit working with the Chinese forces had an interpreter. He was called a "faniguan."

It was difficult taking the wounded back, because it had to be done by stretcher-bearers. They had to go up and down huge mountains, sometimes carrying the wounded for eight to ten days. Chinese communities in that remote sector organized into teams of stretcher-bearers which took part in this work. The precipitous cliffs and gullies were extremely hazardous.

In China the American Medical Corps couldn't do as thorough operating as in Burma where the units were more stationary and therefore more hygienic. They couldn't evacuate wounded by plane because the terrain was so rugged that they had no air-strips. They had to do it with stretcher-bearers. Consequently there was a lot of gangrene.

The American surgical pack trains crossed to the west side of the Salween River—that is, to the side toward Burma—and performed emergency operations on the wounded Chinese who were sent back by litter. These litter cases had to be got across the river on pontoons and boats, and then were carried by stretcher-bearers through the mountains to the field hospitals on the Burma Road leading to the city of Kunming. The reason for this was that the Japanese held the Burma Road right up to the west side of the Salween River and consequently a detour had to be made to get on the highway back of the battle area. Once the wounded were in Chinese-held territory they were evacuated by truck along the Burma Road to the field hospitals.

Our field hospitals worked in conjunction with the Chinese hospitals. The latter were converted temples and ancestral homes, making a very ancient and dramatic setting for the wounded, with the Chinese gods in their niches and the injured men in the cots below. The American field hospitals were set up in regulation Army tents, and in some places they had barracks made of wood.

American Medical Corps forward headquarters was at Panjau, way down on the Burma Road, and medical supplies were sent there by truck from Kunming. The main supply depot was in an ancestral home. Halfway between Kunming and the Salween River was Tali. They would evacuate wounded from the Burma Road by Chinese junk on Tali Lake up to the town of Tali. This junk dated back in type to Marco Polo.

At Paoshan, on the Burma Road, the Friends had an ambulance unit. This was comprised of different nationalities, American as well as British, and cared for the wounded in the same way as the American field hospitals. The Friends got their supplies direct from the British.

Back near Kunming was the rear headquarters of the American Medical Corps. That was where the Fourteenth United States Air Force was, and the main base on the entire fighting front. At Kunming the corps trained the surgeons and GIs who were to make up a portable surgical team. There, too, the horses were taught to carry packs. Here it should be mentioned that the veterinary outfit worked right alongside the Medical Corps in the Burma-China theatre. This was highly important because so much transportation was done by pack-horses.

There were twelve or more field hospitals stationed along the Burma Road between the Salween River and Kunming. In connection with the movement of medical supplies across the Salween from Kunming, there was at one spot on the bank of the river a tiny clearing which was used as a landing field for Cub planes bringing up emergency supplies.

The fighting along the Salween River was in the most rugged terrain imaginable. The convolutions of the earth were fantastic, shooting up to precipices eight to ten thousand feet high, with narrow trails winding in and out. The foliage ranged from scrub pine at the top of the mountains down into the dense valleys of the jungle, with the same threat of disease as in Burma.

The rocks and the precipices would get very slippery from the rain. The horses would lose their footing, and there were times when they would slip over the precipices and drop hundreds of feet. The Corpsmen then would go down and bring the medical supplies back on to the precipices, as it was important not to lose any of the stores.

Once they were across the Salween River they could have supplies dropped to them by plane, but there were cases where American Corpsmen would live on rice alone for days when the weather would prevent planes from coming over. This had a harassing effect on those unused to a straight rice diet, and the Medical Corps was constantly having to replace men because they lost weight and got weak or diseased.

The Burma Road is very rugged. It is an amazing engineering feat, having been carved out of the mountain by Chinese coolies. They blasted sides of the mountains and used the stone for the foundation of the road, breaking the big rocks down until they eventually reduced them to the size of heavy gravel. All of this was done by the hand of the coolie.

It is mostly a two-lane drive, with the great precipices thousands of feet deep on one side and, on the other, huge cliffs jutting up hundreds of feet above you. It winds around the tortuous curves of the mountain like an accordion pleat.

One section had precipices on both sides of the road. You drove along with the feeling of an ant on the edge of a sheet of paper. Trucks would come careening around these curves. It wasn't unusual to see, hundreds of feet below the road, the smashed and charred remains of trucks which hadn't made it. The road was slippery during the rains because clay would be washed down on to it from the mountains, so that you had to drive in low gear.

It was along this Burma Road, in such terrain, that the American field hospitals were stationed. These field hospitals received their freight of wounded and passed it back over this harrowing and dangerous route to the base hospitals at Kunming and vicinity.

At the airfields throughout China where our men were flying either fighters or bombers there was a field hospital set up with doctors and nurses and with complete facilities for operations. In the case of wounded men who had to be evacuated from the air field hospitals to base hospitals, they were flown back by way of Kunming over The Hump to the big base hospital in the Indian province of Assam, or further on to India proper.

All medical corps supplies for China had to be flown over The Hump. Apart from ordinary medi-

cal supplies, the few ambulances had to be taken down completely and in some cases were sawed in half so that they would fit into a transport plane. Trucks were taken down to the smallest possible bit and packed into the planes. There always was danger of supplies running out in China in case bad weather prevented passage over The Hump.

It should be emphasized that despite the primitive conditions under which the U. S. Medical Corps worked in Burma, it was better and more easily supplied there than it was in China—and this notwithstanding the fact that in China the corps operations were far from the fighting front, except for the portable surgical units. This was due to the necessity of flying all the supplies for China over The Hump from India, whereas the supplies for Burma could be taken by road, river or railway for a considerable distance northward through Assam Province from India proper, and then could be flown or carried by truck to the medical unit working at the fronts.

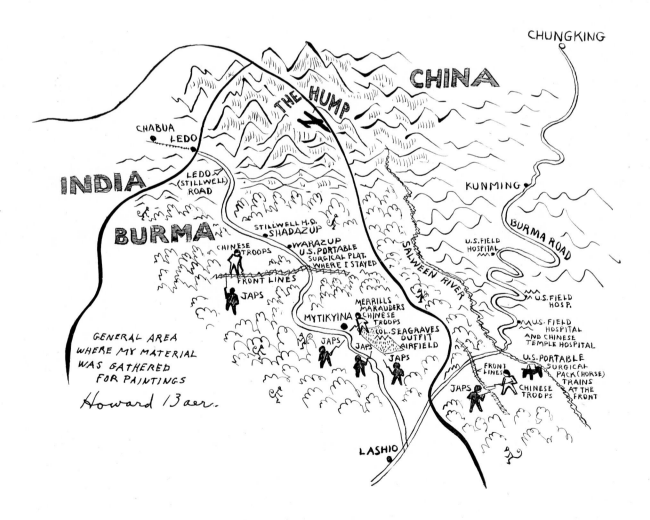

8

The Warrior Comes Home

WE HAVE seen in the preceding chapters and pictures something of the great work done by the United States Army Medical Department in caring for our sick and wounded fighting men in the theatres of war, and in developing preventive measures to safeguard their health. It is a magnificent and unprecedented record.

There is, however, an all-important phase of this which we haven't encountered, except in passing, and that is one very close to the folk on the home front—rehabilitation of the ill and wounded. Rehabilitation aims at the restoration of the earning capacity of the disabled man. But, as the Medical Department points out, this implies more than good medical treatment.

It is not enough to provide medical and surgical care promptly in an effort to save life and to restore health. The corps maintains that there is a larger obligation to ease mental suffering and to restore the individual to a full and useful life. Rehabilitation may be begun in the Army hospitals, but it must be continued after the discharge of soldiers —and it must be helped by the family and friends of the handicapped man.

The vast majority of our boys who have been hurt in battle recover completely. They perhaps bear scars, which serve as handsome badges of honor, but physically and mentally they are as good or better than when they went away to the wars. Possibly their attitude toward life has changed in some ways, but certainly many of them are in better health and have developed poise and confidence.

Unhappily, there is another class which fortune has handled roughly and sometimes brutally. These are the men who have sustained permanent hurts. Despite the swift and highly skilled medical treatment in the theatres of war, wounds sometimes cripple or cause prolonged invalidism, with accompanying distress of mind.

"Often the deepest wounds—those hardest to heal—are of the spirit," we are told by the Surgeon General's office. "It is essential, therefore, that medical treatment attempt to alleviate mental anguish and to supply the information and guidance necessary to insure the handicapped that he can and will be self-sufficient and economically independent.

"Most difficult to dispel is the emotional despair of the blinded, the feeling of aloneness of the deaf mute, or the bitter resentment against a cruel Fate that has allowed one youth to be armless, legless, or otherwise disfigured when so many of his companions suffered comparatively minor discomforts that could be quickly forgotten.

"Initially the disabled soldier shares the common belief that disablement means a complete wreck of all hope for success. Therefore, rehabilitation must combat misinformation and create assurance that life can still be satisfying and successful."

The Army Medical Corps has flung all its tremendous resources into the solution of this complicated problem. The corps has devoted itself to the rehabilitation of every man who possibly can be restored to his place in society.

This reconditioning starts when the wounded man receives his early treatment in the battle zone, or when the sick soldier is hospitalized, and it continues until there is nothing more which medical science can do. The most severe cases, which can't be restored to normal by treatment in the hospitals of the war theatres, are returned to the United States where the fight to rehabilitate them is carried on.

The corps has been able to work miracles, but there is another important factor in the restoration of the wounded soldier and that is the attitude of the people back home. If that is incorrect—if his friends and relatives assume that his case is hopeless and shower him with excessive sympathy—it can do untold damage which all the medical treatment in the world cannot offset.

Surgeon General Kirk, after a tour of European battlefields, made a public statement which went into the subject of rehabilitation and the attitude of the home-front, with the blunt and colorful approach which he employs. He referred to the various steps in handling the wounded, from the firing line to the general hospital in the United States, and compared the evacuation of the injured to "a long conveyor belt." Dealing with the man who had reached the end of this belt in the United States and had been discharged from the Army, General Kirk said:

"He may have lost an arm or a leg. He may have lost both arms or both legs. His face or head may be disfigured. He may be a nervous wreck from battle fatigue and labeled psychoneurotic or psychotic.

But no matter what his condition is, I want to assure you that he will get the best care that medical science can provide.

"All along the line of this medical conveyor belt he has received treatment. His spirit has been developed. He has put his dependence upon the doctors and the nurses. He has seen others with possibly more serious wounds get well.

"He learns to take the loss of an arm, leg, eye or disfigurement, in stride. He believes he will soon be well to do a job and has complete confidence in what the doctors and nurses tell him. That this confidence is not misplaced is shown by the fact that about 97 per cent of those wounded who reach Army hospitals get well.

"The amputee is happy with others like himself. He is furnished a prosthesis (artificial substitute) and taught how to use it. The blinded man is taught to be self-reliant. Plastic surgery takes care of the facial disfigurement. His morale is high. He is ready to face the world. And then what happens?

"When he sees his mother she breaks down and cries. When he walks down the public streets he is the subject of morbid curiosity. When he boards the street car someone tries to help him. These are the things that destroy his self-confidence and the work of months is sometimes undone in minutes.

"The wounded soldier does not want sympathy. Neither does he want charity. Legislation and the grant of funds, embellished by bally-hoo, is not the answer to making him a useful citzen. He wants to be self-supporting and self-reliant. It is only humanitarian to subsidize him in accordance with his handicap, but he does not want pity, gratuities, or sob-sister aid.

"Many of these men when properly trained have a higher earning power than when they entered the Army. They are normal beings and they want to be treated as normal beings.

"Now let us take a look at the psychoneurotic case. First of all the term is widely misunderstood. The public confuses the term with psychosis and immediately labels him crazy.

"There is nothing mysterious about psychoneurosis. It does not mean insanity. It is a medical term used for nervous disorders. It manifests itself by tenseness, worry, irritability, sleeplessness, loss of self-confidence or by fears or over-concern about one's health.

"A great many of these symptoms are manifested by people in civilian life to a greater or less degree. You are all familiar with the chronic complainer. Nearly everyone has some idiosyncrasy about health. In spite of all this, the psychoneurotic in civilian life is not labeled nor does he have difficulty in carrying on his business. Some of our most successful business and political leaders were psychoneurotic.

"But put that successful psychoneurotic business man into the Army and the doctors immediately have a problem on their hands. Our Army is for the most part a civilian army. The majority of our soldiers have had no previous military training. Our citizens have not been regimented. They are used to a beauty-rest mattress and private bath and all of the other conveniences that have made our American way of life so desirable. Some of these men are pampered by over-indulgent mothers and co-workers from early morning to late at night.

"When this type of person is put into the Army he has a lot of adjustments to make. He becomes part of a vast machine that is regulated like clockwork. His job becomes an important part of an over-all job. He is not always in a position to know the ultimate objective of his work, so he starts to worry about it.

"He has other adjustments to make. There is mass feeding. Often he is on K rations. Sometimes he has no rations and he has to shift for himself. There is mass sleeping and the man next to him snores. Unfamiliar sounds disturb his sleep. On maneuvers he has to sleep on the ground, and on the battlefront he may not get any sleep for hours at a stretch. These are all disturbing elements to him.

"Under all of these conditions it is difficult for him to adjust. It's hard enough for a rugged, hardy individual to adjust, let alone a man with psychoneurotic tendencies. Therefore the nervously inclined individual who was a success in civilian life, fails in the Army and receives a discharge.

"We also have the moron, the mental defective and the constitutional psychopath to deal with. We get the alcoholic, the pathological liar and the pre-criminal in the Army. We have the boy who has been a failure all his life. He is a problem child at home and his school and occupational records have always been poor. Very few of these men ever make good soldiers.

"Then we have the nearly normal individual who cracks under combat. Everyone has his limit of mental and physical endurance. A man can stand just so much. Put him in combat and under prolonged shelling and bombing, combined with poor rations, sometimes none at all, and he becomes a casualty.

"It's not the first time strong men have broken down after giving what it takes!

"We may have as many of this type of casualty as we do physically wounded, and the cycle of medical care for him starts immediately. If he does not return to active duty within a reasonable time after treatment he is brought back to the United States and after reconditioning may be discharged.

"Reconditioning consists of three phases—physical, educational and occupational. All patients in the Army Service Forces hospitals are included in the program except those acutely or seriously ill. The bed patient is given orientation and education in addition to physical bed exercises or occupational bed handicraft. As he increases to a ward ambulant stage, these activities are intensified. The program is progressive through all stages of convalescence and balanced so that no one phase is over-emphasized. Thus, if he is to be discharged, he is ready to undertake the occupational training offered by the Veterans' Administration or go into his former job.

"The most important thing which friends and relatives of the disabled veterans can do is to treat them naturally—treat them as normal men. Attention should not be forced upon them. People should not shudder at their afflictions and they should not be gushed over.

"These men are hypersensitive. If they have lost an eye, or an arm or a leg they may feel, if friends or relatives unwittingly encourage that feeling, that the bottom has dropped out of the world they knew. But that isn't true. We all know men and women who have successfully overcome grave difficulties and have lived useful lives.

"Give him some sympathy, sure. The injured man needs to know that his family and friends care for him. That is very important. But they must also know that this soldier is no longer 'a boy' except to his mother who will always think he is, and he should not be so treated.

"Through training and leadership, he was, when wounded, a soldier—a soldier who could give and take—lick the best the enemy could offer. In other words he was a courageous, mentally and physically fit man. Don't ever let him lose this fighting spirit.

"The wounded soldier must be allowed to do things for himself. If he finds he can tie his own tie, or lace his own shoes, it is much better that he do it than that it be done for him. He must discover that, despite his handicap, he can do these and other things to give himself confidence and self-respect.

"Parents, relatives and friends should not attempt to minimize the results of his injury. They must be realistic and honest. They should not tell him that he looks fine when he doesn't. But they can tell him he'll soon be as good as new.

"These wounded and disabled service men have no desire to be martyrs. They don't want to be treated as heroes. They have rendered a great service to our country. They have made a great sacrifice.

"So a great responsibility rests on the public. Public behavior has got to be adjusted so that by ill-considered actions additional handicaps are not placed upon the disabled soldier. On the other hand, by intelligent understanding of their problems and needs the public can help them along the road to success and happiness."

Men needing physical reconditioning certainly have every reason to hope that excellent results will be achieved, owing to the tremendous advance in medicine and surgery as a result of war experiences. For example, take deformities of the face which are the cause of so much mental distress to the injured man. New and better procedures have been developed in plastic surgery, and disfigurements are almost totally eliminated in many cases. The same thing holds true of other blemishes—say of the hands.

Then there is the man who has lost a limb, or perhaps two. Artificial limbs are being made so amazingly well that many users of them can hold their own in a great diversity of jobs with men who have no physical handicap. Moreover, following the suggestion of Surgeon General Kirk, the National Research Council set to work to create artificial limbs superior even to the very excellent ones at present in use. These new prosthetic appliances are expected to be the best in the world.

The number of men who have been blinded in both eyes fortunately is comparatively small. Where one eye has been lost we have the new artificial eye mentioned in a previous chapter. This is made from acrylic resin instead of glass and is a great improvement over the old type. It is much lighter, fits perfectly and—best of all—is very life-like.

For each of those who have suffered the grave disability of total blindness, the Army provides medical care and surgery by specialists, a vocational training program and a chance for further education. The Valley Forge General Hospital, Pennsylvania, and Old Farms Convalescent Hospital, Avon, Connecticut, are representative centers for the rehabilitation of blinded veterans. Delicate operations restore sight to some of the boys, but those who are beyond this type of help are educated so that they will be able to gain the skill and confidence whereby they can adjust themselves to their new life.

This educational work is carried out not only by aides who have normal eyesight but by others who are totally blind and have overcome their handicap. The sightless soldiers are taught to see with their minds and hands. This helps them to conquer the fears which beset them when first they are plunged into total darkness. As a matter of fact they acquire an acuteness of the remaining senses which may even make them superior in some respects to the person who can see.

The objective of the educational course is to remove the blinded man's five fears—fear of darkness, fear of failure to be accepted by family and friends, fear of moving about, fear of impaired earning power, and fear of being unable to occupy his spare time. One of the first things in the education of the newly blinded patient is to teach him such simple things as arranging toilet articles, shaving, telling the time with Braille watches, and finding his way about the hospital. Much of this teaching may be done by a blind man. The student naturally doesn't learn his lesson without some knocks, for in trying to move about he runs into obstacles or blind comrades, but all this is met in a spirit of banter which bolsters morale.

As soon as the blinded man passes the preliminary stage of adjustment he is sent home on furlough to get re-acquainted with the relatives and friends whom he can't see, and with familiar haunts. After that experience he is taken back to his training center to continue his education. This includes such things as the reading of Braille, touch typewriting and craft work. This rehabilitation course is being enlarged.

There is another program for men who have been deafened. This is compulsory, whereas after the last war it was on a voluntary basis, and so the afflicted man isn't permitted to resume the battle of life in the midst of that terrible loneliness which surrounds those who cannot hear.

There are three centers specially provided for handling the deaf. These are the Deshon General Hospital at Butler, Pennsylvania; the Borden General Hospital at Chickasha, Oklahoma, and the Hoff General Hospital at Santa Barbara, California. Army doctors say the program represents the most hopeful attack ever made on the problems involved in deafness.

All types of the most up-to-date hearing devices are available so that the patient may be fitted by scientific tests. For those who are beyond such mechanical aid the first thing the doctors have to do is to overcome the defeatist psychology of deafness and make the patient understand that his handicap definitely can be mastered.

Among other things a new method of teaching lip-reading has been initiated. The patients are shown motion pictures of such common incidents as a man making purchases in a grocery store or sitting down to a meal with his family. These movies help the lip-reader to take in a situation as a whole. Most men are fairly proficient in lip-reading by the time they have covered the short basic course of some 35 lessons which run half an hour each.

These are a few of the highlights in the physical and psychological rehabilitation of the war veteran. This rehabilitation has been characterized by Major General David N. W. Grant, the Air Surgeon, as "the greatest challenge which faces the medical profession today." General Grant also has given us a striking message which he feels "that the physician, the relatives, the friends, the employer, and the community of the war veteran should hear." Speaking with special reference to the air corps, but in terms which apply equally to any fighting man, General Grant says:

"Whether he (the war veteran) is labeled a neuropsychiatric casualty, or is discharged for some other reason, or is merely home on leave, any differences in his behavior probably comprise a hangover from his normal reactions to an abnormal way of living and dying.

"What war has done is call upon this individual to accept the abnormal idea that self-preservation is less important than self-sacrifice—that there is a distinction between killing a man in peacetime and killing him in war. Conditioned throughout his formative years to seek security and comfort, to love peace and freedom, the raw recruit is quickly and brutally exposed to a system which, first in training and then in combat, subordinates his personal security to that of the group, continually replaces comfort with hardship and strain, offers him peace only as the distant reward for making war, and denies that freedom is preferable to authoritarian discipline and regulation.

"It is difficult for the individual to adapt himself to this military deflation of his ego, to this superimposition of the group ego on, and frequently against, his will. All men are alike in that they have feelings and in that these feelings may run into emotional conflict with other feelings which are equally acceptable.

"Can these soldiers who have faced tensions and stresses far beyond any peacetime demand upon their organism be regarded as mentally suspect because they carry the anxieties they have developed in combat back home with them? You know the answer is no.

"These men have been poured into a mold, the mold of war, and to remove them from it requires adjustments as profound as those they were forced to make when they changed from civilian to military environment. They present all degrees of difficulty in adjusting to the peaceful, prosaic and trivial circumstances of home life after learning to live in a fighting group which so orders their life that it can give all or take all with one word from one commander.

"One man—flexible, resilient—may come home, take his wife on a fishing trip and settle down to being 'good old Bill' again without so much as a harsh word. Things are different, but he can 'sweat' anything out. Another high-strung race-horse of a man perhaps finds that the releases he found in combat are boiling over in hostility toward his mother's solicitation, or in a desire to punch the nose of every civilian he sees on the street.

"This is the challenge we face each time a war veteran returns home—to see that he has full opportunity to spring back to his original personality curve.

"Given a little time, and a little help, most of them will."

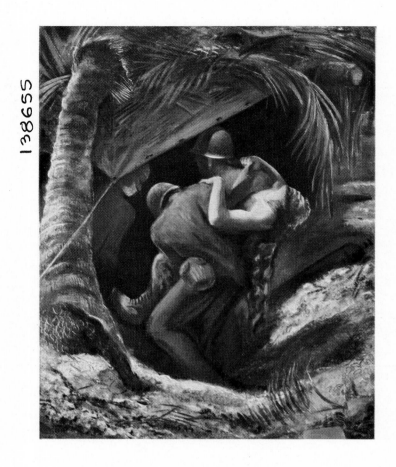

PAINTINGS

of

MEN WITHOUT GUNS

1. **JUNGLE—ALLY OF THE ENEMY**—Franklin Boggs. *The tropical jungles of the South Pacific are aligned on the side of the Japs. Infested with malaria, strange tropical fevers and skin diseases heretofore unknown to the occidental world, these jungles constitute a formidable barrier protecting our Japanese enemies. When they are not busy attending wounded men, the medics move around through the jungle with a bottle of solution and a swab, checking the ravages of prevalent skin disease.*

3. PACIFIC BLACK DIAMONDS—Franklin Boggs. *These men of New Guinea played an important part in the evacuation of the wounded and the rescue of downed airmen. Their uncanny ability to traverse the dense jungles rapidly and stealthily and their innate kindness meant the difference between life and death for many a veteran of South Pacific fighting.*

NIGHT DUTY—Franklin Boggs. *An Army [nurs]e breaks the monotonous vigil of night duty by mak[ing] a check on a coughing patient. Artist Boggs slept in [the] ward in the South Pacific—was struck by the eerie [effect] of a flashlight's beam on the green mosquito nets [whic]h shroud the sleeping wounded. He reported: "The [night] sounds of the jungle cannot be painted, but are [never] unforgettable."*

4. PILL CALL—Franklin Boggs. *Soldiers suffering from malaria get their daily quota of atabrine tablets from the Medical Corps captain. Artist Boggs caught this scene in the South Pacific. The temporary coloring of the patients' skin, he explains, is "more vivid than that of the enemy who controls the quinine."*

5. END OF A BUSY DAY—Franklin Boggs. *Bloodstained litters give mute and shocking testimony of the fierceness of the struggle—gruesome evidence of a busy day for the bearers of wounded and dying men. Washing these litters in the salty water of the South Pacific—salt water does the best cleansing job—is one of the many unpleasant chores assigned to enlisted men of the Medical Corps. But litters must be clean for tomorrow—and more men.*

6. FRONT-LINE SURGERY—John Steuart Curry. *Highly mobile surgical teams attached to field hospitals have made front-line surgery a reality in this war. Blood plasma, the sulfa drugs and penicillin are great life-savers, but Major General Norman T. Kirk, the Surgeon General of the Army, says they are "essentially adjuncts to the prime requirement—skilled surgeons qualified to apply the latest and most modern techniques."*

7. COLLECTING STATION—
John Steuart Curry. *After hasty examination and emergency treatment at the Battalion Aid Station, which is right behind the battle lines, wounded men are brought to the Collecting Station, a mile or more to the rear. Here they are given additional emergency treatment pending another trip to the rear to the Clearing Station. This picture was found by the artist at Camp Barkeley, Texas, where Medical Department tactical units are trained.*

8. **STEEL COFFIN**—Fred Shane. *A wounded man in a burning or stalled tank is in a desperate plight. It is not easy for able-bodied men to make a hurried exit from a disabled tank under fire—almost impossible for a badly wounded man. At the Medical Department's Field Service School, Carlisle, Pennsylvania, the "medics" are taught how to lift an injured soldier from a land battleship. The Medical Corps is explaining the rescue techniques to the bleacherites. Note the special harness used to lift the "casualty" through the conning tower opening. Newer tanks have escape hatches near the bottom, simplifying the getaway.*

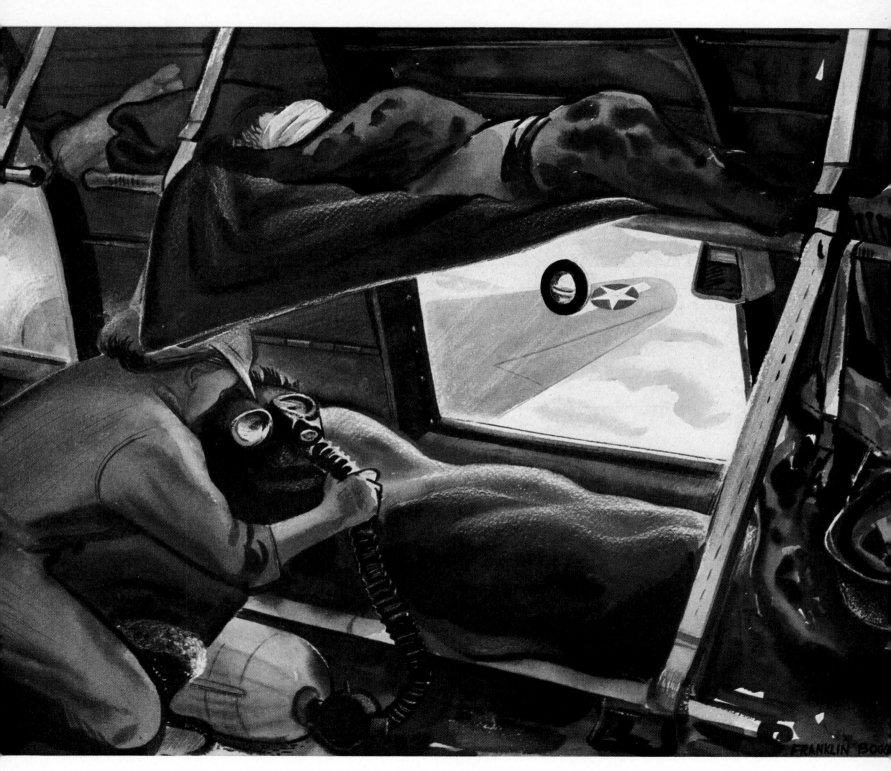

9. **AIR EVACUATION**—Franklin Boggs. *High over the Owen Stanley mountains a flight nurse administers oxygen to a wounded soldier. The plane is bound for Australia, next stop on the long journey to the United States and a general hospital near home. Only hours before, this same plane had arrived in the battle area with a load of ammunition or medical supplies.*

10. **RETURN TO THE GOLDEN GATE**—Franklin Boggs. *Wounded men aboard an Army transport crowd the rail for the first joyous glimpse of the Golden Gate Bridge. The excitement on deck quickly pervades the entire ship, and from a ward below decks a paralyzed patient succumbs to the infectious gaiety of his buddies, hitch-hikes topside on the sturdy back of a corpsman. These ships are outfitted with operating room, dental clinic —amply provided with medical supplies and adequately staffed by Army doctors and nurses.*

11. **RACE AGAINST DEATH**— Franklin Boggs. *In this Japanese pill-box site on Admiralty Island, which but a few hours before had been spouting death and injury, Army doctors have set up a front-line emergency operating unit. Artist Boggs' brush conveys the devastating tempo of invasion warfare. Crisis, speed, grimness, reality, mercy are registered here in rapid bewildering succession.*

12. SOUTH SEA ISLAND PARADISE—Franklin Boggs. *Stately palms swaying gently in the breeze, eternally green foliage, white sandy beaches kissed by warm chameleon waters, straw-skirted hula girls—the average American pre-war conception of life in the South Pacific. This 1944 version by Artist Boggs features uprooted, broken palms, a discarded plasma bottle, bloodsoaked bandage, empty first-aid tins and spent syrette—signs of mercy once meted out by men of the Medical Corps.*

13. THE AMERICAN WAY—Franklin Boggs. *A frantic, bewildered mother dogs the footsteps of a Medical Corpsman in the Admiralty Islands as he carries her wounded child away from the combat area. Emergency treatment has been given at a Battalion Aid Station—more definitive care at the hands of expert Army doctors will follow.*

14. **UP TO DOWN UNDER**—Franklin Boggs. Wounded Australian soldiers are being loaded aboard a big Army transport plane for the long flight over New Guinea's Owen Stanley mountains to the land of the kangaroo. Thousands of wounded Americans and Aussies were evacuated by air. Crude flying fields and incessant tropical rains added greatly to the evacuation problem.

15. SOUP'S ON—Fred Shane. Mess halls and dishes are left behind when Medical Department soldiers go on maneuvers at the Army's Field Service School in Carlisle, Pennsylvania. It is just as important that they learn how to get their chow on the fly as it is that they master the art of handling "wounded" under battle conditions. This lieutenant displays fine technique in the presentation of his mess kit and cover to the K.P. dishing out the groceries.

16. TIME OUT FOR CHOW—Fred Shane. Medical Department soldiers at the Army's Field Service School, Carlisle, Pennsylvania, grab a bite during war maneuvers. These men carry no guns—are armed only with emergency bandages, sulfa, and pain-relieving drugs. It is their job to pick up wounded men, almost as soon as they are hit, and rush them back to waiting Army doctors at Battalion Aid Stations.

17. **HIDING OUT**—Fred Shane. *Somewhere at the "front" at the Medical Department Field Service School, Carlisle, Pennsylvania, medical soldiers in training cover their ambulance with camouflage netting. This is a rendezvous spot, and here the ambulance will wait until litter-bearers bring back the "wounded" for a fast ride to Army doctors.*

18. **QUICK TREATMENT**—Fred Shane. *This is a Battalion Aid Station right behind the "front" at the Medical Department's Field Service School, Carlisle, Pennsylvania. The "wounded" soldier is getting emergency medical attention preliminary to his removal to a Collecting Station farther back where more advanced treatment will be administered. The Army's medical soldiers at Carlisle are thoroughly trained—know just what to do when they get into action.*

19. MEDICAL SUPPLY DUMP—Robert Benney. *It was very thoughtful of Hirohito's little men to leave this spacious dugout undamaged when they departed for their Japanese Heaven. The great Pacific outdoors isn't the best place in the world to store perishable medical supplies, so this ready-made emergency storeroom came in very handy. Artist Benney visited this medical hideout while at a Pacific island base.*

20. "EASY, JOE"—Robert Benney.

21. SICK BAY—Robert Benney. *While aboard an invasion-bound ship in the South Pacific Artist Benney paid a visit to the sick bay. The ship's doctor prescribes for minor ailments—keeps the men in good shape for the landing soon to come.*

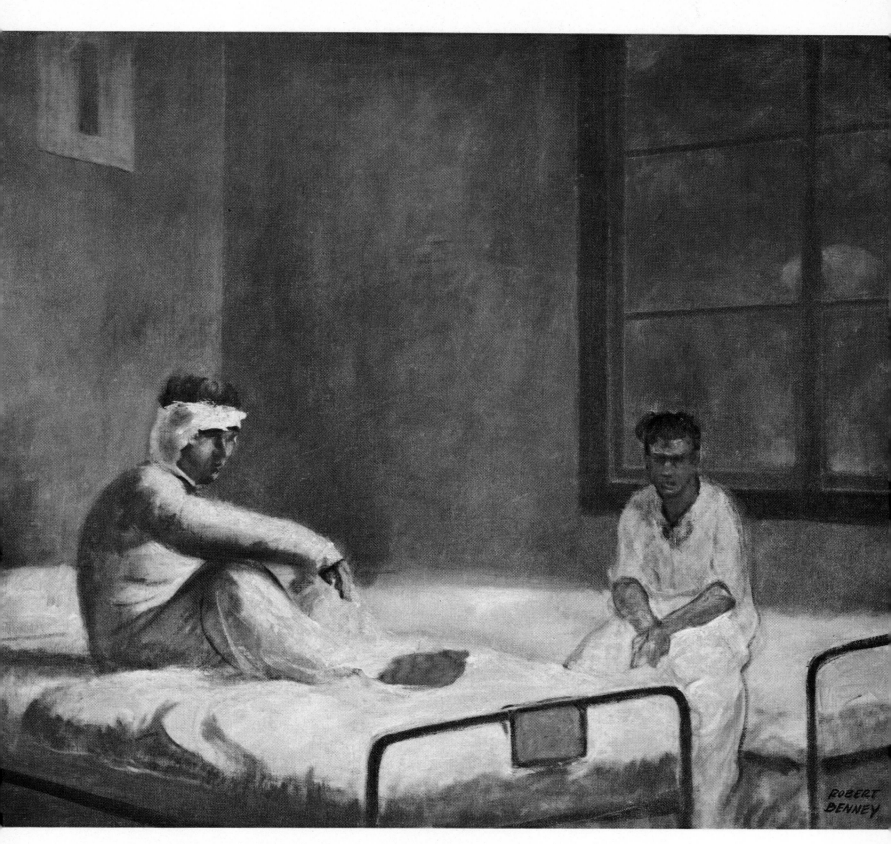

22. PACIFIC BASE HOSPITAL—Robert Benney. *In sharp contrast to the hastily constructed and highly maneuverable medical units of front-line combat, are the numerous rear echelon hospitals scattered throughout the vast Pacific. Here, in the cool and quiet atmosphere far from the battle, a man has time to reflect, while his wounded body is made well and strong again.*

"...we had to leave Frank, he got it in the leg."

23. SAIPAN, JULY, 1944—
Robert Benney.

24. JAP COMPOUND IN SAIPAN—
Robert Benney. *An Army doctor bandages the head of a Jap civilian in Saipan while other subjects of the Mikado line up for medical attention.*

25. NORMANDY VICTORY CARGO—Lawrence Beall Smith. *When the LST's returned to the English ports of embarkation, they carried wounded from the Normandy beach-heads. In order to avoid the enormous confusion of two-way traffic at the docks these ships were met by the smaller LCT's out in the harbor. The ships were "married," and litter bearers transferred the casualties. When an LCT was filled, it headed for the beach and waiting ambulances.*

26. SUNDAY IN NORMANDY—Lawrence Beall Smith. *Enlist-
men of a Collecting Station of the First Army "digging in" next to a chur
in a tiny village near St. Lo. Little was left of the burned-out village wh
this outfit arrived. The men were kept busy during periods of heavy activ*

setting up tents, treating the wounded and evacuating them by ambulance
to clearing stations in the rear. Shortly after Artist Smith reached the spot,
the Germans counter-attacked from their lines 800 yards distant, and all
equipment and wounded had to be removed rapidly.

27. RETURN CARGO—Lawrence Beall Smith.
The huge tank decks of the LST`s *were carpeted with litter cases when they backed off the Normandy beaches for the dash back to the white cliffs of Dover. Weather, mines and German "E" boats impeded the progress of the ships, and sometimes wounded men spent many long, miserable hours aboard before reaching the comparative safety of England's shores.*

28. LABORATORY WARFARE—Manuel Tolegian. *The Army Medical Department's war on disease is constant and unrelenting. The Army's laboratories are the battlefields, with Army doctors and nurses pitted against germs, microbes, and other pathogenic bacteria. Artist Tolegian's brush found this picture at Camp White, Oregon, former training center for members of the Army Nurse Corps.*

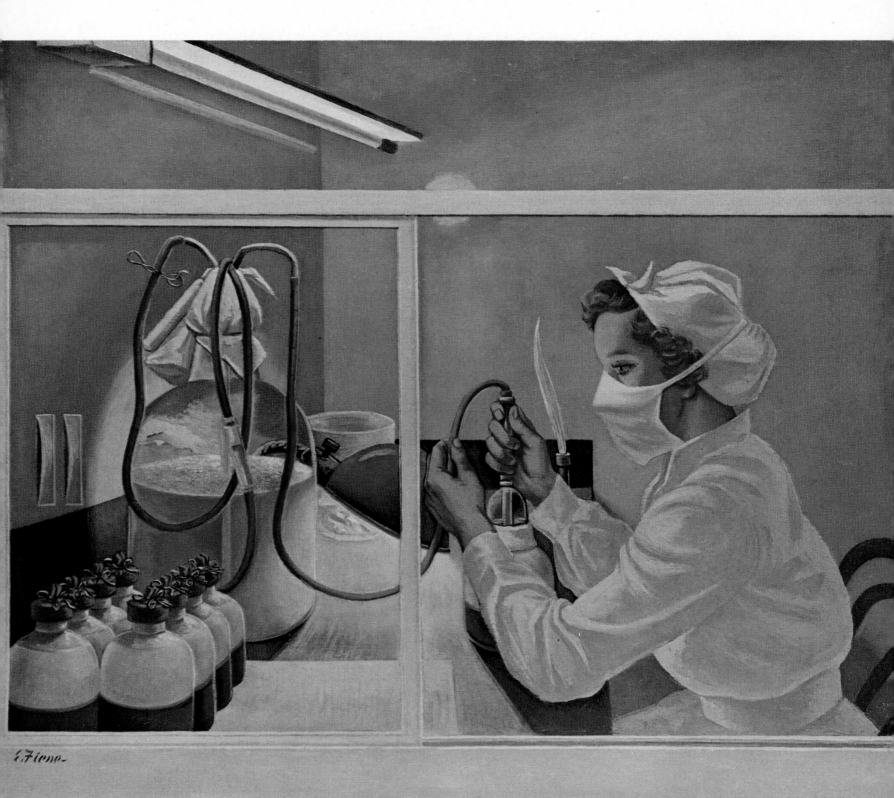

29. LIFE-GIVING PLASMA—Ernest Fiene. *Blood plasma has been one of the foremost lifesavers of World War II. Artist Fiene's brush brings this picture from one of the great laboratories where plasma is processed for the Army Medical Department. The technician is drawing off the plasma from the blood cells. It is a delicate operation, performed under the strictest aseptic conditions. Dried plasma must be free from all blood cells and any contaminating bacteria. The small bottles in the foreground show the plasma at the top, the blood cells (dark) at the bottom.*

30. JUNGLE TRAIL—Franklin Boggs. *Through the unfriendly, tightly-knit New Guinea jungle an Army Medical Corps unit threads its tortuous way inland, loaded down with the back-breaking components of a portable hospital. The black, tousled heads of the jungle-wise natives bob evenly along in striking contrast to the bended backs and bowed helmets of the corpsmen. Units like this crawled for endless, miserable days over the Owen Stanley mountains.*

31. EVACUATION UNDER FIRE—
Franklin Boggs. *Immediately after driving the Nips from entrenched positions on this Admiralty Island hillside, a Medical Corps unit set up this Battalion Aid Station in the sheltering scarp of the sharp-rising knoll. Men on the ridge dig in for protection against the stubborn Japs who give ground grudgingly. Wounded in the back and pelvis, the man on the incoming litter seeks relief from his painful injuries by kneeling.*

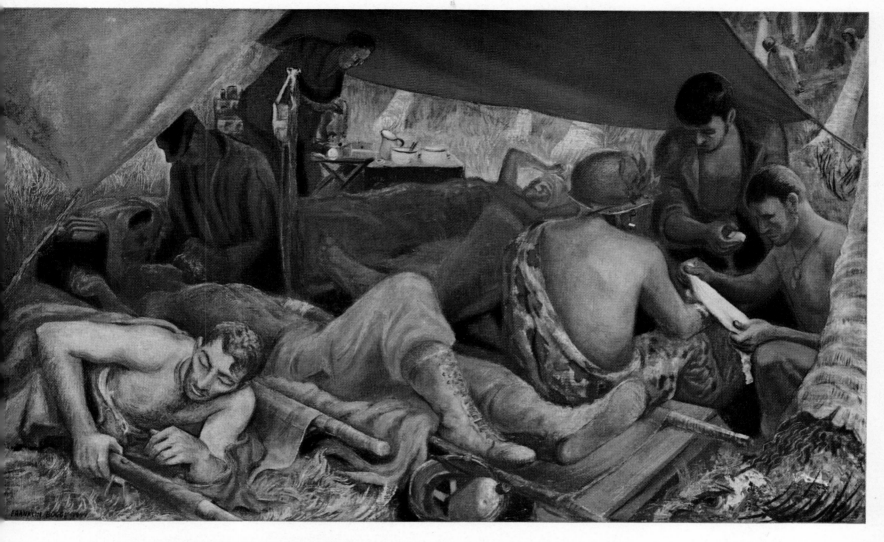

33. BATTALION AID STATION—Franklin Boggs. *The men pictured here by Artist Boggs are receiving emergency treatment at a front-line Battalion Aid Station (Papa Toli Mission, Admiralty Islands) a few minutes after being hit. One man is getting plasma while another has his arm bandaged and treated with sulfa. In the lower left a wounded man tries to lift himself up in his litter as the effects of morphine begin to wear off.*

ANOPHELES HOME FRONT—
...klin Boggs. *Breeding grounds of the Anopheles ...uito in New Guinea are invaded by a Sanitary ...s Officer and squad of energetic grass-cutting na... The Anopheles is the carrier of malaria, formid... ...nemy of American troops in the tropics. The Army ...cal Department wages ceaseless, untiring war ...st malaria—not the least important phase being ...ol of mosquito breeding areas.*

34. NATIVE CASUALTY—
Franklin Boggs. *A New Guinea native gets some American emergency treatment after being injured by a falling upright during the construction of a hospital ward. They were willing workers and of immeasurable help to the Seabees and Army Engineers.*

35. VISITING HOUR—Franklin Boggs. *In the early phases of the New Guinea fighting, native houses were used as hospitals for wounded and sick men. Civilization has no monopoly on kindness to the sick. This native brought flowers every day to his new-found American friends.*

36. TRAIN FARE—Robert Benney. *Believe it or not, it's ice cream! Just one of the delicacies served to our wounded men while they travel across the country on one of the Army Medical Department's Hospital Trains. This careful study by Artist Benney betrays the indelible imprint of war on the boy's face. A year ago, perhaps, a dish of ice cream would have brought a smile to youthful eyes—not now.*

37. SHORT CUT TO LIFE—Robert Benney. *The lives of many wounded men in Saipan were saved by the fast diagnoses of this front-line X-ray unit, working in an abandoned Jap shack. In the cases of severely wounded, the difference between life and death was measured in seconds. This fast-moving unit turned out an X-ray plate every two minutes. The Army doctor studies an X-ray of a man who is on his way to the operating tent, as two other wounded men await their turn on the X-ray table.*

38. HOSPITAL TRAIN CHEF—Robert Benney. *The boys do not have to be introduced to the train's jovial cook. They just know that his name is "Skinny"—and that's what they call him. "Skinny" typifies the kind of chow he serves—nothing but the best for the best.*

39. NIGHT RENDEZVOUS—Robert Benney. *Somewhere on the cold, wind-swept plains of Kansas, the Hospital Train keeps a tryst with waiting ambulances. Swiftly, quietly, carefully, wounded men are transferred from the train to the ambulances for the trip to one of the Army's great General Hospitals. Light for the work at hand is provided by the automobile headlights which knife their way through the blackness. Through unsympathetic clouds, a frustrated, faltering moon tries to lend a hand—tries to send a message of cheer and hope to unhappy men.*

40. NIGHT VIGIL—Robert Benney. *While the Hospital Train through the lonely night, the Army nurse checks the patients' charts. S of the wounded men sleep soundly—others fitfully. To some the rhyth clickety-clack of the speeding wheels is a sweet lullaby to their harde shell-blasted ears—to others a relentless reminder of barking machine g At the far end of the car, the medical aidman keeps an alert eye on precious cargo.*

ROBERT BENNEY

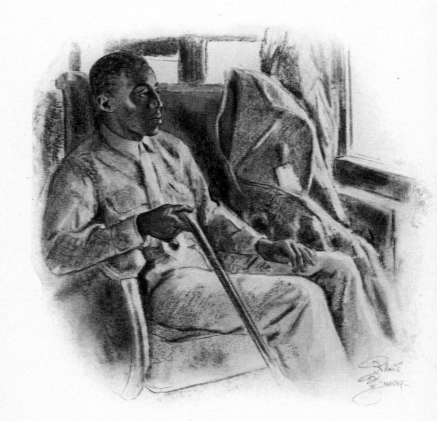

41. COMING HOME—Robert Benney. *Every turn of the Hospital Train's wheels brings this convalescing soldier nearer to home and friends. For him, there have been many days at the front, many more in the hospital. A gentleman and a soldier, he carries a cane involuntarily, but it will steady the faltering steps of a new leg.*

42. CLIMATIC CASUALTY—Robert Benney. *Through the narrow doorway of an isolated compartment aboard the Hospital Train, Artist Benney saw this GI victim of a respiratory disease, one of many who are unable to withstand drastic changes in climate and living conditions. He is a casualty not of the enemy's making in the strictest sense.*

43. WOUNDED ABOARD—Lawrence Beall Smith. *Doctors, Medical Corpsmen and ambulances are present for the "sweating in" of the returning mission. Coming in late in the day and often in the heavy weather which hangs over Britain, any ship in the group which has wounded men aboard will drop red flares so that medical aid will be on hand the minute the ship taxis to a stop.*

44. DEATH OF A B-17—Lawrence Beall Smith. *At dawn on a cold March morning, a B-17 took off on a long mission to Germany. It crashed on the yellow field of an English farm just a mile and a half away. Ten men were blown to bits—all ten were on their first mission. For hours, the doctors and Medical Corpsmen carried out the miserable and sickening job of human salvage. Artist Smith adds the following to his canvas: "Though the explosion of three one-thousand-pound bombs jolted us heavily back at the base, the hay stacks, windmill, and trees were left undamaged adding a macabre touch to the scene. The fire was started by one of the engines hurled through the woods."*

45. RETURN FROM MISSION—
Lawrence Beall Smith. Wounded member of a Fortress crew finally removed from the ship after the tortuous return from mission. The only spot of color is the heated suit, called a "blue bunny." The electric cord attached to the suit is rather symbolic of the man's complete break with the lung machine of which he was an integral part for ten hours.

46. HOSPITAL BOUND—Lawrence Beall Smith. The removal of wounded from the air base by ambulance to the nearest station hospital was carried out in a very short space of time. Here casualties are leaving from the medical stations at the air base. A farmer plows his field nearby. The cloud of smoke is from burning oil on one of the Fortress "hardstands."

47. NORMANDY WASH—Lawrence Beall Smith. The field hospitals, usually four to eight miles behind the lines, were often the scenes of contrast such as this caught by Artist Smith's brush. Families moved back into their shattered towns after the battle passed to live amid Army installations of all kinds. French children loitered around field hospitals asking for chewing gum for themselves or cigarettes "pour papa." They carried flowers—either as a friendly gesture or as a medium of exchange.

48. FIRESIDE COMFORT—Lawrence Beall Smith. *Housed in Nissen huts, the station hospitals at the many English air bases were well equipped to care for wounded airmen fortunate enough to get home on a wing and a prayer. The little English stoves kept the huts comfortable, and groups such as this one depicted by Artist Smith hovered over many firesides.*

49. SNOOKER—Lawrence Beall Smith. *Playing a game called Snooker at the Red Cross Club of a station hospital. This subject had an amusing pool room atmosphere.*

50. "MEAT WAGON" POOL—Howard Baer. *Jungle Garage—Motor pool of ambulances in Burma jungle, Portable Surgical outfit "Meat Wagons" are what the boys call them.*

51. BURMA MUD—Howard Baer. *Army Medical Department ambulance bogged down on a Burma jungle trail during the monsoon. During the rainy season many trails became impassable for ambulances and medical supply vehicles—supplies had to be moved forward by pack trains and on the backs of native carriers.*

52. AMBULANCE, JUNGLE STYLE—Howard Baer. *Chinese stretcher bearers in elephant grass, Burma jungle. Sometimes these men carry the wounded as long as eight days before they can be hospitalized. You can't over-estimate their endurance and courage.*

53. SCANT SHELTER—Howard Baer. *Chinese Medical Aid Station at the front lines in Burma jungle within rifle and mortar fire range. Chinese stretcher bearers carrying wounded in background.*

54. JUNGLE CHEATER—Howard Baer. *Baby Piper Cub plane takes aboard a wounded man at a small clearing in the Burma jungle. These small planes can get into and out of jungle holes with the agility of a bird. They fly wounded men to surgical installations in an hour, spanning mountain and jungle trails that it would take native litter bearers two weeks to traverse.*

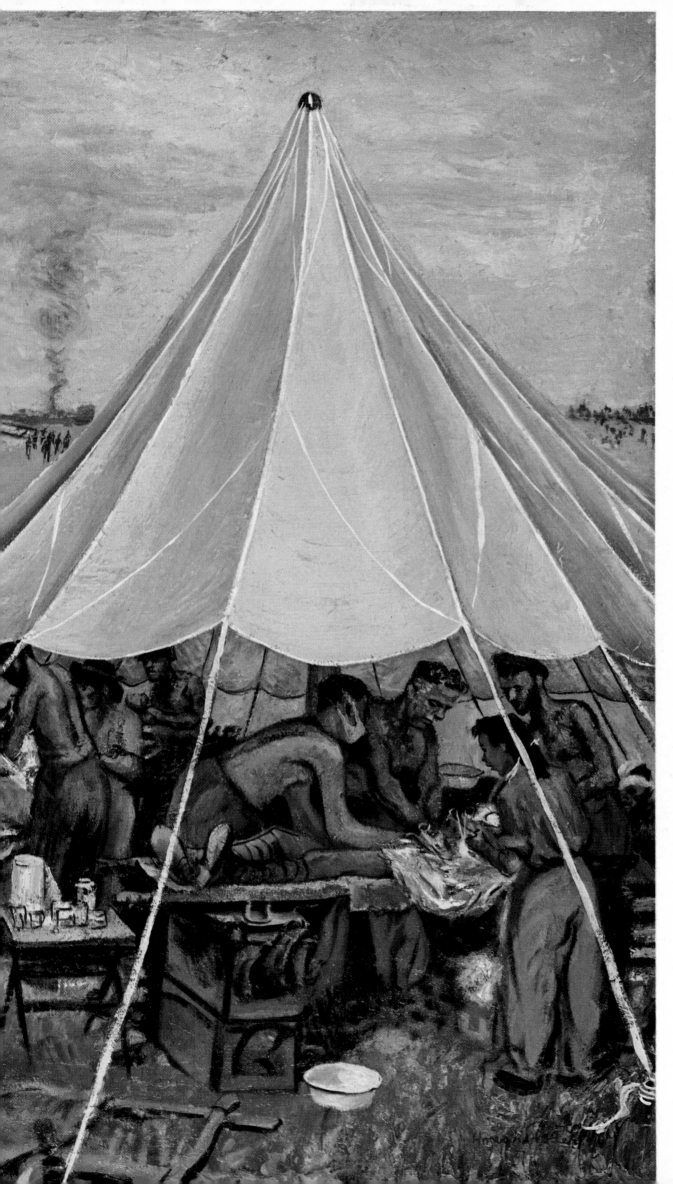

55. FIELD HOSPITAL IN TECHNICOLOR — Howard Baer. *A few hours before Artist Baer came upon this scene at Myitkyina Airfield these colored parachutes, pitched as tents, floated from the skies with ammunition, food and medical supplies. Each type of supply has its own distinctively colored chute. Troops have taken the airfield, but the Japs still infest the jungle brush around the edges. So Burma Surgeon Seagrave found it practical to pitch his parachute tents on the airstrip. As he operated (foreground), assisted by Burmese nurses whom he had trained, American fighter planes overhead kept the Japs in the surrounding brush reasonably quiet.*

56. MOON-LIGHT IN BURMA—Howard Baer. *Army doctors operate on wounded American soldiers through the hot Burma night in a ceaseless, tireless struggle to save lives. The lush Burma foliage provides a perfect asylum for this forward-area Portable Surgical Unit, but a moon-lit sky is no help. Army surgeons attached to these portable units often operate continuously for 18 hours.*

57. JUNGLE HOSPITAL—Howard Baer. *Evacuation hospital in North Burma jungle. This is the only hospital which has American nurses in the Burma jungle. They do an excellent job.*

58. ARTIST'S MODEL—Howard Baer. *Wounded American tank man. "I found that all the American wounded at the front showed no surprise at finding an artist, and were completely cooperative when asked to pose, doing so with no self-consciousness," says Baer.*

59. **OPEN-AIR SURGERY**—Howard Baer. *Reception tent, Portable Surgical outfit, Burma jungle.*

60. **AID STATION**—
Howard Baer. *Parachute tent, Medical Aid Station, Tank Unit, Burma jungle.*

61. MESS CALL—Lawrence Beall Smith. *Station hospitals in England were housed in many Nissen huts. Ambulatory patients walked from their ward to the Mess Hall carrying their own coffee cups. This hospital was set in a wooded section, and the noise of the cook's oven competed with the constant roar of planes leaving and returning from nearby bases.*

62. AMATEUR EDGAR BERGEN—
Lawrence Beall Smith. *This youthful patient in the Orthopedic Ward of a station hospital in England was an air casualty and as such had lots of company. He was somewhat unusual, however, in that he was an amateur ventriloquist who kept the whole ward amused by putting words into the mouth of the tiny doll suspended over his bed. Here he is playing "bingo" with the other men in the Ward in a game directed by a Red Cross girl.*

63. **PACK TRAIN IN CHINA**—Howard Baer. *Medical Department pack train bridges the mountain wilderness which lies between American forces on the Salween River front and supply depot at a nearby air base. Narrow ledges along the cliffs of the river canyon make hazardous, stubborn trails which exact a heavy penalty for a single misstep. Even the sure-footed, little Chinese horses must be coaxed and cajoled to carry on. Encumbered by heavy loads of plasma, sulfa drugs, penicillin and other medical supplies, the animals must be guided carefully by the corpsmen.*

64. DYING WOUNDED SOLDIER,
SALWEEN FRONT, CHINA—
Howard Baer.

65. CHINA LIFE LINE—Howard Baer. Chinese
stretcher bearers, familiar with mountain trails and
masters of the rugged terrain bordering upon the Burma
Road, carry American wounded from the Salween front.
The litters are a native product, crude but comfortable.
The crosspiece spanning the litter handles shifts some of
the load from the arms of the bearer to his broad, stout
back.

66. CHINA SUPPLY RENDEZVOUS—Howard Baer. *Nestled in the deep gorge of the Salween River, guarded and sheltered by mountainous overhanging cliffs, this tree-rimmed maidan is an ideal supply relay site. Tiny Piper Cubs bring food, medicine and other supplies to the Medical Department pack trains which continue to Salween front over precarious ledges skirting the river canyon. The Cubs do not require large areas for landings and take-offs—get away from this Salween oasis by flying upriver through the chasm in the background.*

67. JUNGLE WARD—Howard Baer. *After operation by a Portable Surgical outfit in the Burmese jungle, the wounded rest in a ward tent awaiting evacuation to field hospitals.*

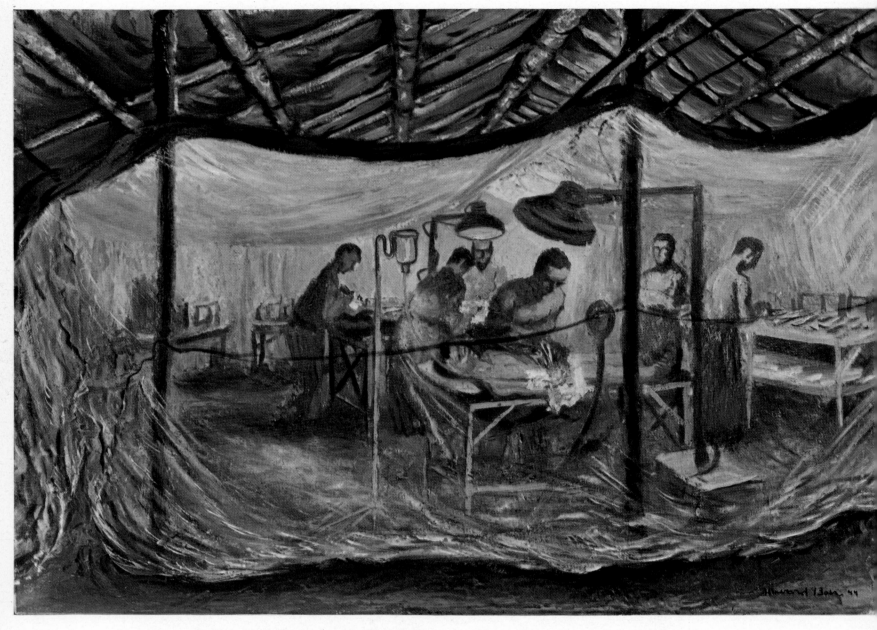

68. JUNGLE OPERATING ROOM—Howard Baer. *Medical Department surgeons of an advanced field hospital in Burma lose no time in operating on wounded men to save an arm or a leg—or life, itself. The Surgeon General has ordered that there shall be no delay in giving men surgical attention because he knows that early surgery means a low mortality rate. Artist Baer found this jungle field hospital in a native "basha" completely enclosed by netting to protect patients from mosquitoes and other disease-laden tropical insects.*

69. TANK CASUALTY—Howard Baer. *American tank corps officer burned in engagement, Burma jungle.*

70. **NIGHT OPERATIONS**—Howard Baer. *Operating at night, Burma jungle, Portable Surgical outfit.*

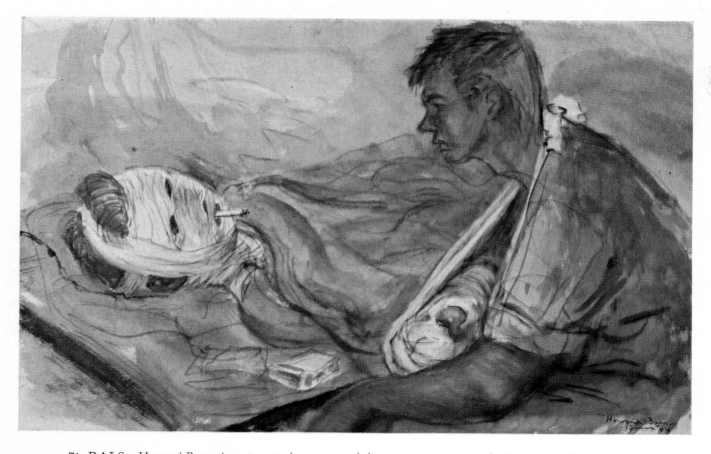

71. **PALS**—Howard Baer. *American tank man wounded in an engagement in the Burma jungle, coming out of anesthesia; buddy also wounded in same engagement watches anxiously.*

72. FRIENDS AMBULANCE UNIT—Howard Baer. *This unit, affiliated with the Chinese Red Cross near Pashan, is down on Burma Road around 650 km. mark.*

73. CASUALTY (a)—Howard Baer. *Chinese wounded by Jap officer's saber, receiving drop anesthesia.*

74. CASUALTY (b)—
Howard Baer. *Debridement of wound; clearing away scar tissue.*

75. CASUALTY (c)—
Howard Baer. *Anesthetized patient bandaged and carried by stretcher with center hole to fracture table. Stretcher is suspended by straps until series of straps are attached to patient. Then stretcher is lowered to ground. This fracture table was designed by Col. Seagrave in Hakawng Valley, Burma.*

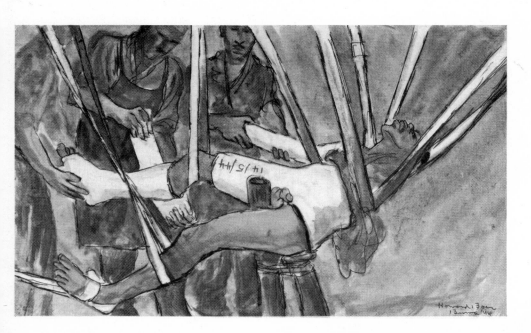

76. CASUALTY (d)—
Howard Baer. *Patient is being bandaged with plaster rolls in order to immobilize the tissues for evacuation to base hospital. This is done to prevent hemorrhage during transit.*

77. CONVALESCENTS—Howard Baer. *Chinese wounded after operation, under overhanging mosquito nets.*

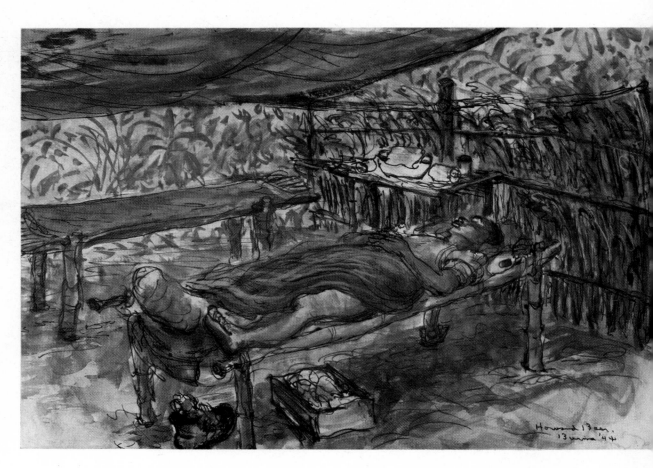

78. JUNGLE PATIENT—Howard Baer. *Waiting for the surgeons, Burma jungle, Portable Surgical outfit.*

79. SELF-SERVICE IN SAIPAN—Robert Benney. *Ambulatory patients wait upon themselves at this Saipan patients' mess visited by Artist Benney. They have to wash their own mess kits, too. In the foreground two wounded soldiers enjoy an after-lunch siesta.*

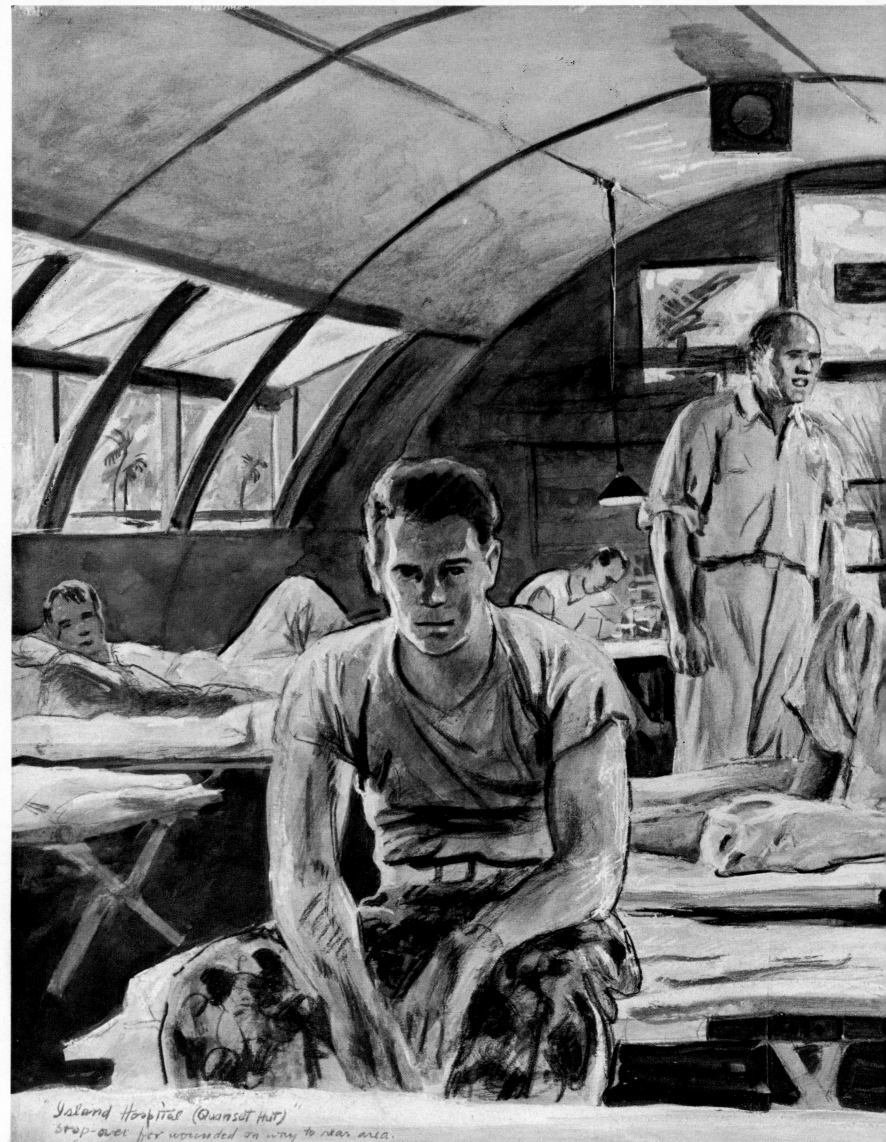

"Island Hospital (Quonset Hut)"
stop-over for wounded on way to rear area.
ROBERT BENNEY Eniwetok — 7/44

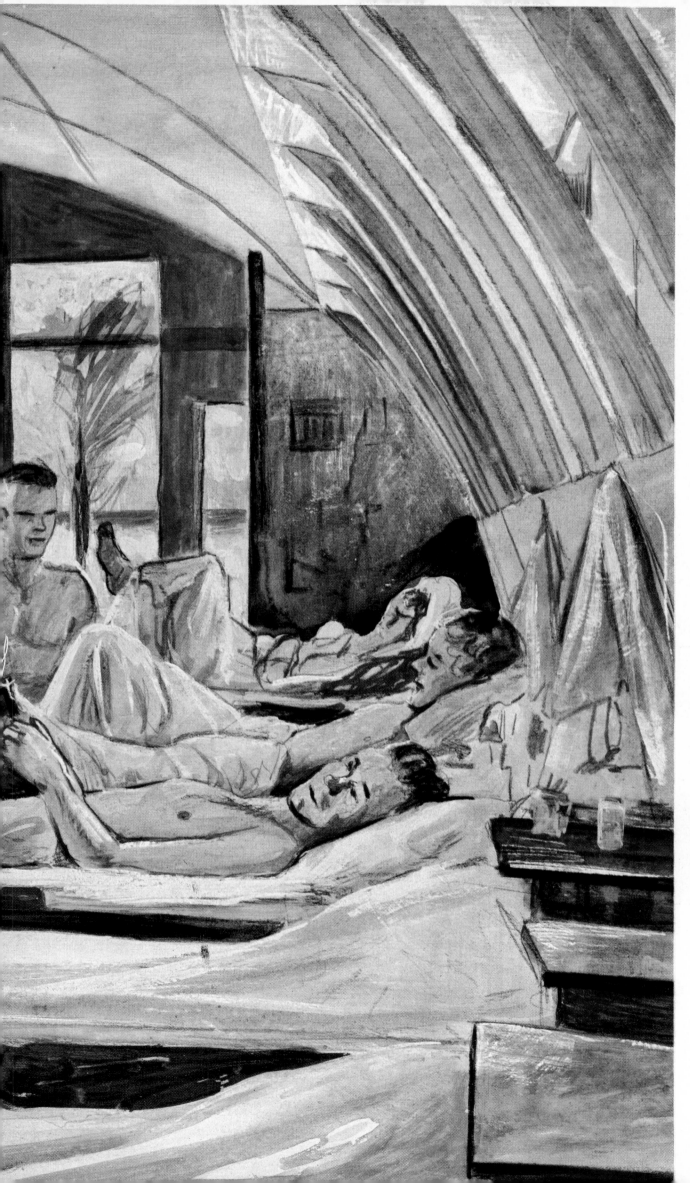

80. ISLAND HOSPITAL—
Robert Benney. *Somewhere in the
South Pacific Artist Benney found
this cheerful, neatly-turned Quonset
hut. It was a stop-over spot for
wounded men headed for base hospital in the rear.*

81. **JUST OFF THE LINE**—Robert Benney. *This man has just been brought from the front line to a Collecting Station. Although wounded less than an hour before, he has received medical attention three times. He was given emergency treatment on the battlefield, had a splint put on his arm at a Battalion Aid Station, and received a special dressing on his thigh at the Collecting Station. Next stop to the rear is the Clearing Station, and more treatment.*

ROBERT BENNEY

82. **TANK AMBULANCE AT SAIPAN**—Robert Benney. *An amphibious tank brings a load of wounded from an "alligator" aid station, near the remains of the city of Garapan, to waiting LST. What our own guns did not destroy at the Battle of Garapan and Hill 500 was taken care of by the Japs, who applied the torch lavishly before giving up their capital. The utter exhaustion of the wounded men makes them seem indifferent to the violent scenes of destruction so recently left behind.*

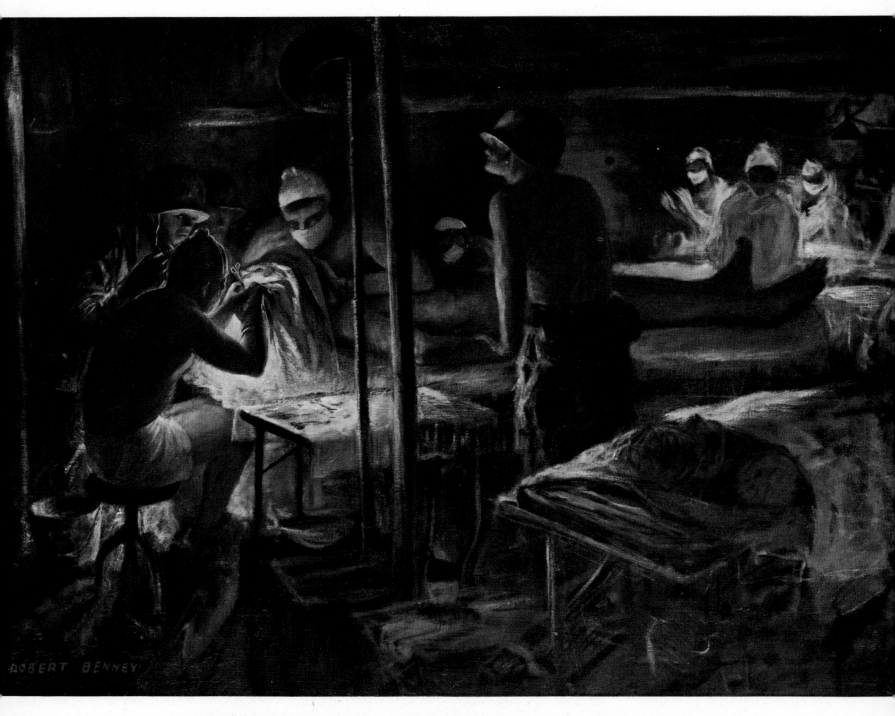

83. FLASHLIGHT SURGERY IN SAIPAN—Robert Benney. *Army doctors performing a delicate brain operation continue doggedly by flashlight during a Jap plane raid on the hospital area. All power was shut off when the raiders appeared, plunging the hospital buildings and tents into Stygian darkness. In spots like this the pocket flashlight is as important as the scalpel.*

84. SAIPAN CASUALTY—Robert Benney.

85. FRIEND IN NEED—Robert Benney. An
American Red Cross representative in Saipan listens
to a tale of woe from an American soldier far from home
—makes notes while the GI tells his story. In all probability the soldier is too busy fighting Japs to write home,
has asked the Red Cross man to get a letter off for him.
Red Cross field workers in combat areas do much to
comfort our fighting men.

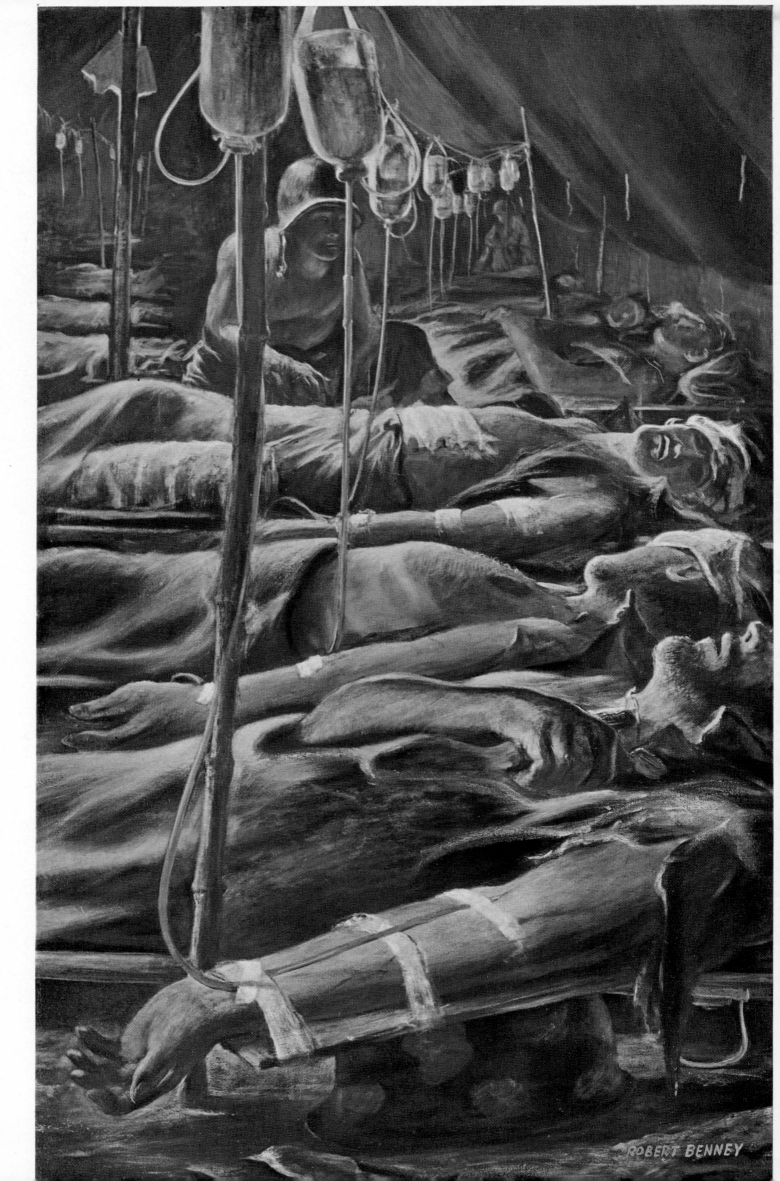

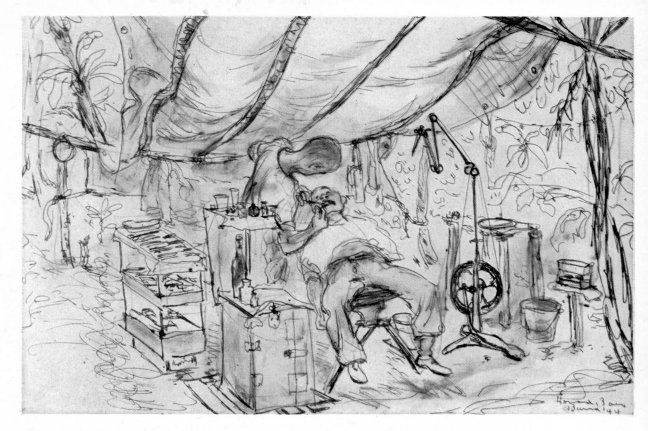

87. "OPEN WIDE"—Howard Baer. *Dental set-up, Portable Surgical outfit, Burma jungle.*

...HOCK TENT—Robert Benney. *The seriously ...led as well as those suffering battle fatigue are im- ...tely taken into the shock tent where plasma is con- ...y being administered during the tide of battle. At ...as many as 40 or 50 men will receive plasma at ...me time. The great thrill of seeing these men ...ht back to life as the blood from fellow Americans ...nds of miles away slowly drips into their veins is ...t never to be forgotten, says Artist Benney.*

88. JUNGLE VET—Howard Baer. *Debridement of shrapnel wound, U. S. Army Medical outfit with Stilwell's forces in Burma.*

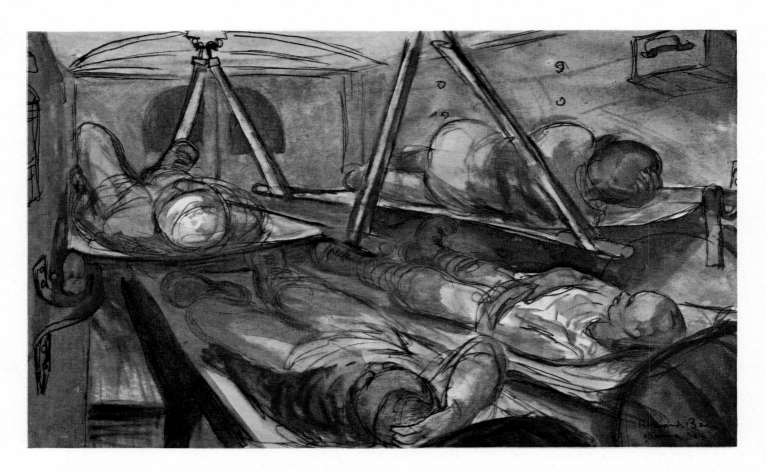

89. **OVER THE BUMPS**—Howard Baer. *Wounded men in ambulance being carried from aid station at the front in Burma, to Portable Surgical outfit for operations.*

90. **BURMA AIR AMBULANCE**—
Howard Baer. *Sick and wounded men being evacuated by plane from the Burma fighting to a base hospital in Assam. Their wizened scrawny bodies and forlorn faces reflect the wretched existence from which they flee. Many of the flight nurses on these unarmed planes were former airline stewardesses—pretty, brave, devoted to duty. Japanese Zeros and obscure mountain peaks combined to make this run a hazardous business.*

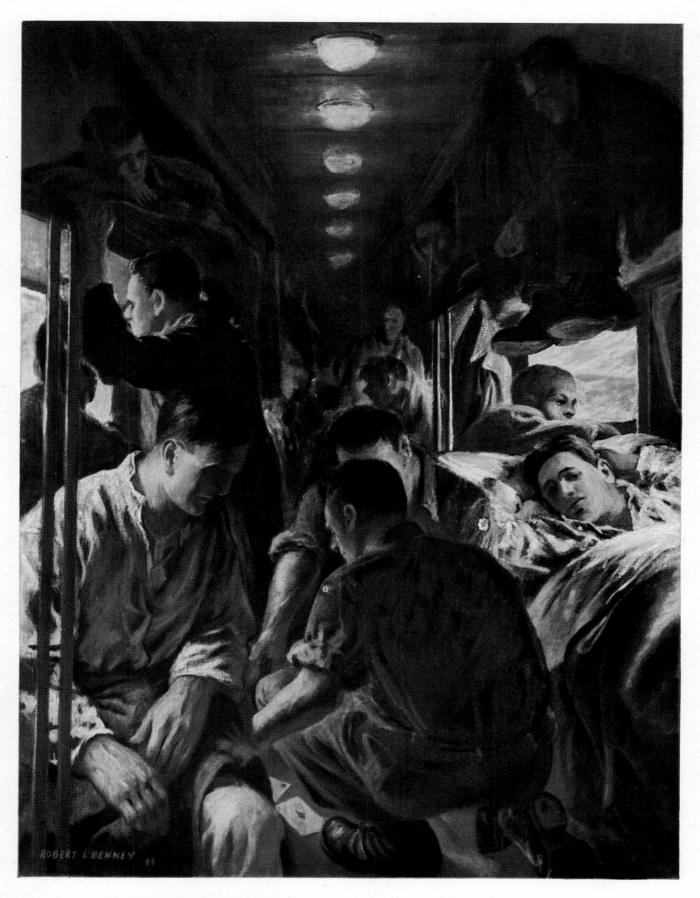

91. **DOUBLE DECK OF ACES**—Robert Benney. *The Ace on the floor is an eloquent bill-of-lading for this car of the Hospital Train and its load of wounded soldiers. Artist Benney's brush has run the gamut of emotions in this daytime scene. The card game has its kibitzers in choice upper tier seats. Down the aisle, men swap combat stories, and at the window, a colored hero looks thankfully at the good old U. S. A. landscape—home. In front of him, a badly wounded man just looks—and wonders.*

93. NURSE IN NEWFOUNDLAND—Joseph Hirsch. *Army nurses on duty wherever there are American troops are writing a glorious chapter in the history of World War II. Of this rustic winter scene, Artist Hirsch has this to say: "There is nothing glamorous about the work the nurses do in Newfoundland; this nurse is going to her post at 6 A.M."*

WAYLAID—Robert Benney. *This band of patriotic home-front
ricans waited long hours for the Hospital Train to arrive at the rail-
operational stop where coal and water are taken by the locomotive.
though the train larder is spilling over with fine food, the wounded
eagerly accept the homemade cakes and sandwiches from the family
ns of the kindly, simple townfolks. After all, Mother's cookies were
s best.*

95. TALKING IT OVER—Howard Baer. *Buddhist temple converted into Chinese hospital 424 miles from Kumming. Adjacent to the American field hospital, where patients undergo operations.*

THE WAY BACK—Lawrence Beall Smith.
*scene portrayed here by Artist Smith was enacted
y times after D-Day. Evacuation of casualties by
was accomplished successfully despite vicious at-
s by enemy planes. This LST at Omaha Beach dis-
ed tanks, trucks, men and supplies from her fiery
th, and before the dust, smoke and gases from the
rted machines had cleared, the long procession of
r cases and walking wounded filed into the ship for
trip back to England.*

96. **MAKING TYPHOID VACCINE**—Francis Criss. *The Army produces its own typhoid vaccine in its laboratories. It began developing typhoid vaccine in 1909, has pushed forward relentlessly since in building its defense against typhoid bacillus. Army laboratories are capable of producing 1,500,000 doses in a single week! During the Spanish-American War, 14,000 out of every 100,000 soldiers contracted typhoid fever; in World War I, only 37 men in every 100,000 got typhoid—in this war, typhoid is practically nonexistent.*

97. SHOULDER WHEEL—Francis Criss. *Physical therapy used in reconditioning of the wounded soldier takes many forms. The apparatus shown is a Shoulder Wheel. It is used for strengthening and developing the long muscles of the shoulder and arm. These muscles may have become atrophied from disuse during convalescence. At the beginning of the treatment, the wheel runs freely—but as the muscles gain strength the tension is increased.*

98. FRACTURE WARD—Peter Blume. *A more complicated*
ject could scarcely have been selected by the artist. It is a study in
pure mathematics with triangles predominating. Beginning with a
triangles as represented by the ceiling, floor and walls, the artist has
imposed other geometrical figures as represented by the fracture or "B

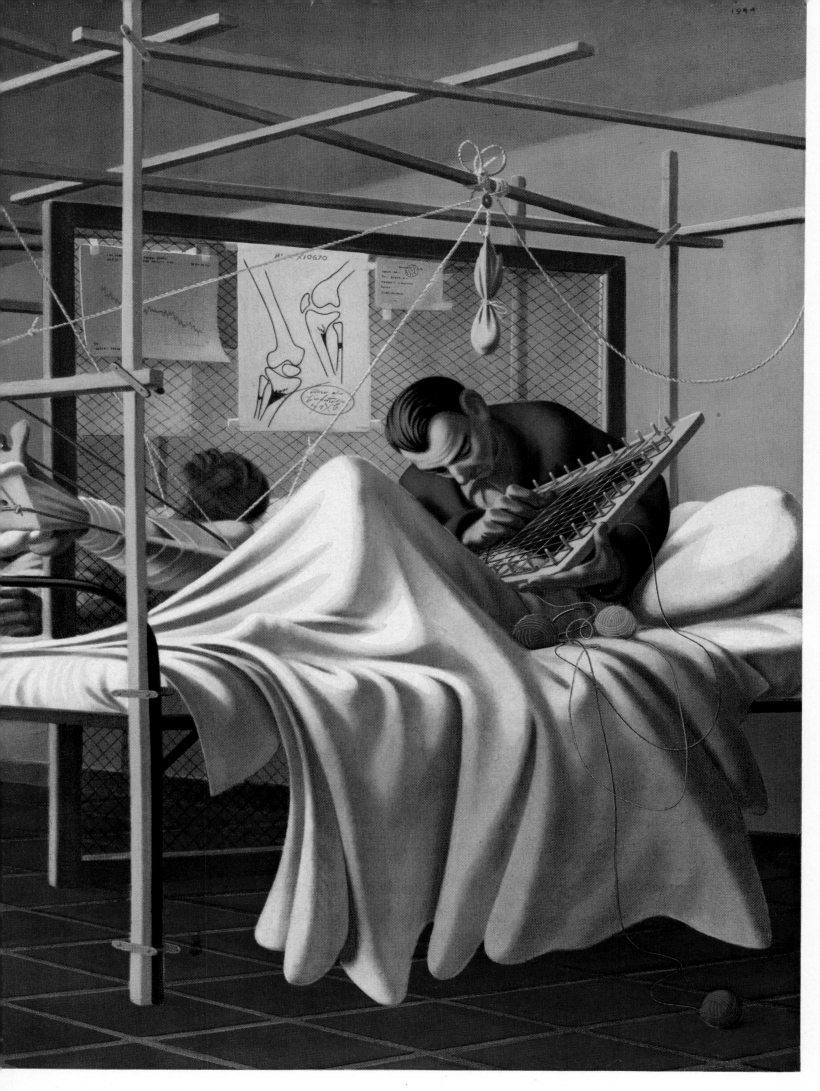

," and then not satisfied, has superimposed the traction cords. In
ds of a lesser artist, such a task would result in confusion, but
ume has achieved clarity, definition, and has presented a fine record.
ndling of the drapery is especially interesting, and the bright colors
bring the composition into harmony rather than to further confuse it.

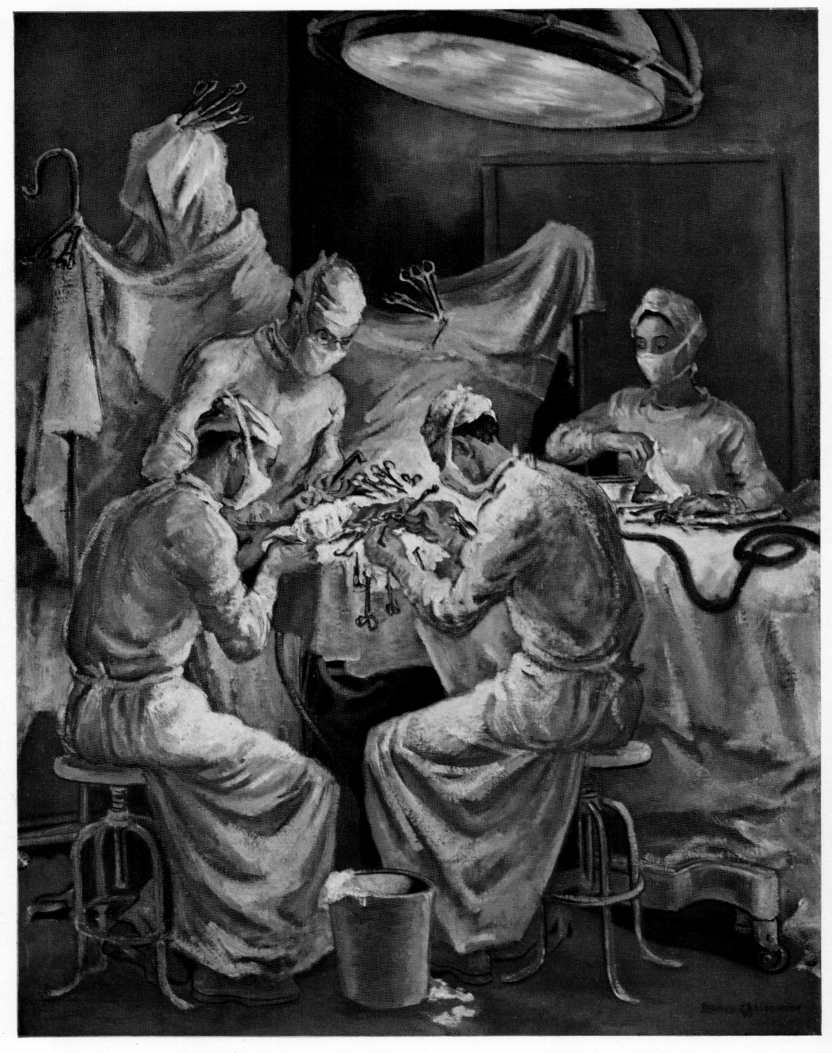

99. **NEURO-SURGERY**—Marion Greenwood. Army surgeons at the Medical Department's England General Hospital, Atlantic City, perform a delicate nerve operation on a soldier who was severely wounded by shrapnel in the European fighting. The severed ulnar nerve is being spliced to overcome paraylsis of the arm.

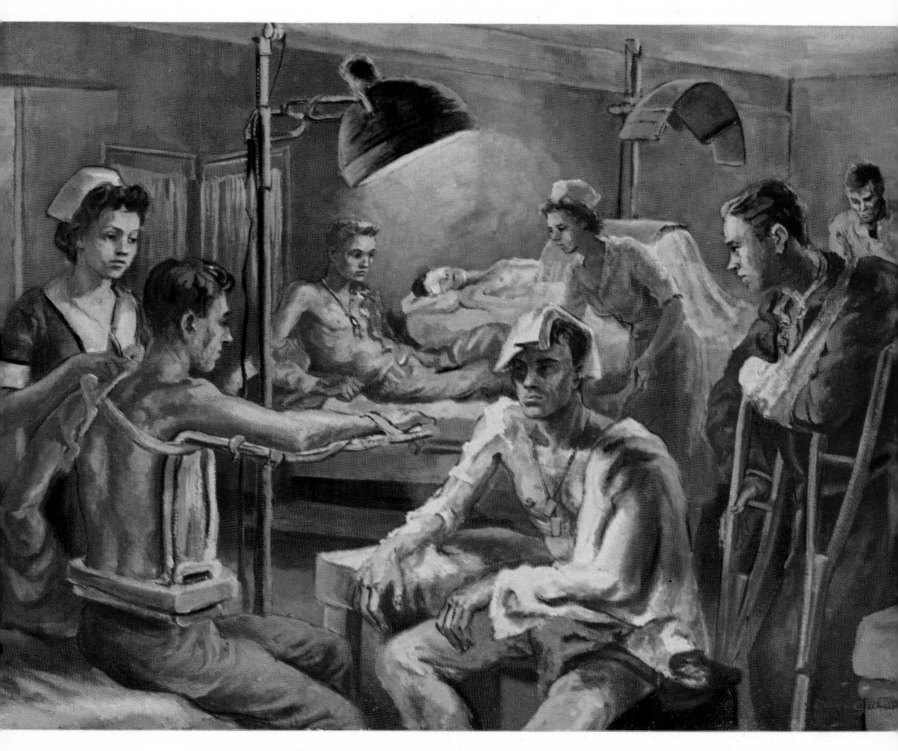

100. **SPEEDING RECOVERY**—Marion Greenwood. *Physical therapy plays an important and early part in the restoration of American wounded, particularly those suffering from injuries to muscles, joints, bones and nerves. It follows closely upon the heels of surgery—keeps muscles and tendons pliable while crushed or severed nerves are being revived to feed them with energy and control.*

101. BEER FOR TWO—Marion Greenwood. *Wounded soldiers undergoing treatment at England General Hospital swap combat yarns over a quart bottle of beer at the PX (Post Exchange). The hospital PX is well-stocked also with candy, ice cream, cake and assorted tidbits At the counter an Army nurse gets an impromptu report from a Medical Corpsman.*

102. **THE QUICK AND THE DEAD**—Lawrence Beall Smith. *The once painful and slow litter haul by foot from Battalion Aid Stations is still painful, but thanks to the versatile jeep, is now mercifully short. Through shell-torn roads still under fire, these vehicles make the trip back to the comparative safety of the Collecting Station in a few minutes. The carcasses of dead cattle in the field and hedgerow ditches near St. Lo contributed a mute, grim, and grotesque comment on man's ingenuity.*

103. TENSION AT DAWN—Lawrence Beall Smith. *The Flight Surgeon is "on the line" for the always dramatic take-off for mission over the Continent. One of the great dangers is explosion on take-off. Flame from an engine, even though usually temporary, is an unwelcome spot of color against an English dawn.*

104. WOUNDED CREW MEMBER—
Lawrence Beall Smith. *First aid treatment of wounded crew member of Flying Fort immediately upon return to base. This man was given emergency treatment by crew members in the air.*

105. PERSONAL MAGNETISM—
Joseph Hirsch. *The galvanic principle of a mine detector is here applied in the form of a foreign body locator which expedites finding bits of shell fragments in the flesh.*

106. HOSPITAL FOR ALLIED WOUNDED—Joseph Hirsch. *An entire evacuation hospital in Africa was given over to the care of wounded soldiers from armies of our allies. In this picture French Moroccans while away the time playing checkers. They proved themselves extraordinarily brave in the North African fighting— worried more about losing their precious queues than their lives, for the hand of Allah lifts a dead Ghoum to heaven by his queue.*

107. HIGH VISIBILITY WRAP—Joseph Hirsch. *The Army doctor left two very important openings in this head bandage. The neat triangular window gives the soldier good vision, and there is plenty of room for the all-important cigaret.*

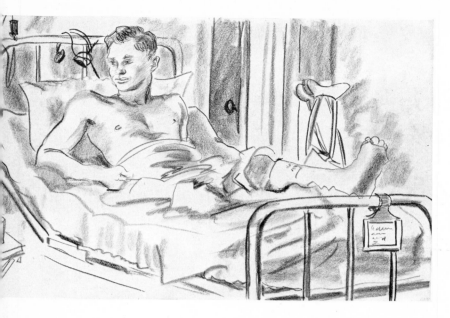

108. WOUNDED BOY—Marion Greenwood.

109. **THE DENTAL FRONT**—Marion Greenwood. *There can be no doubt in the minds of these wounded men at England General Hospital but that Sherman was right. With battlefields and enemy guns behind them, they line up again for assault from an unexpected quarter. Miss Greenwood has caught the utter dejection written upon their faces. But healthy teeth are reflected in a man's general physical condition. When a man is kept in good shape during convalescence, recovery is faster.*

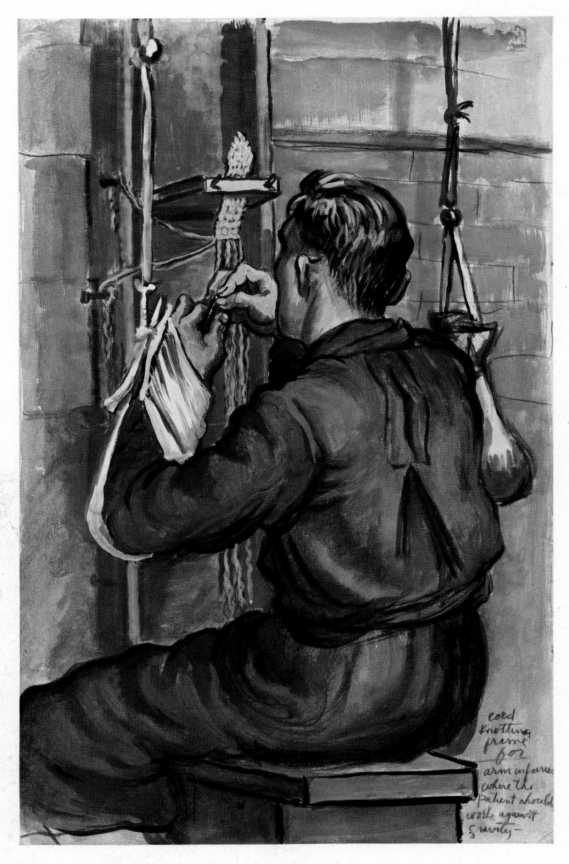

110. **OCCUPATIONAL THERAPY**—Marion Greenwood. *With the aid of a special apparatus designed to exercise his injured arm, this wounded man weaves a belt. Occupational therapy plays important part in the rehabilitation of physically incapacitated veterans. By keeping the disabled man's mind occupied and off his infirmity while teaching him a craft in a skillful manner, occupational therapy serves a twofold purpose.*

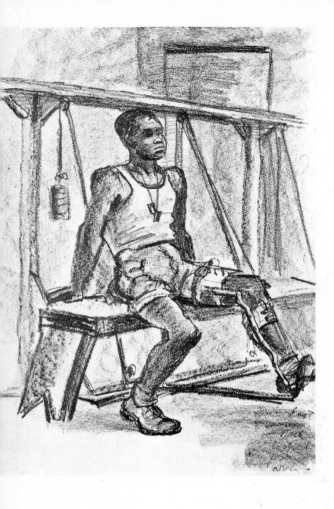

111. **LEG WORK**—Marion Greenwood. *Advanced Reconditioning. Pulley exercises for injured and paralyzed limbs.*

112. **WOUNDED MAN WITH CRUTCHES**—
Marion Greenwood.

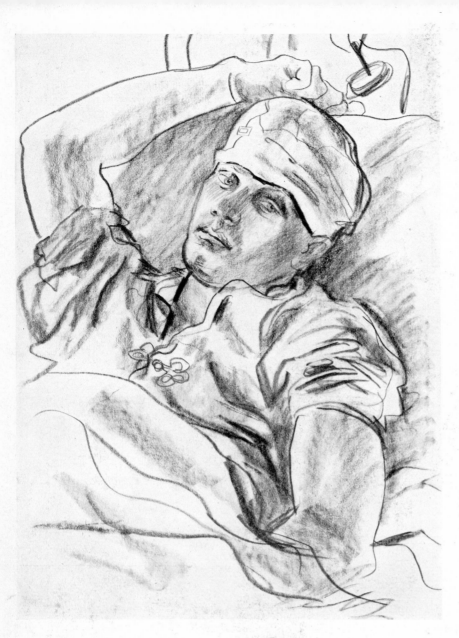

113. **HEAD WOUND VICTIM**—
Marion Greenwood. *Study of soldier after brain opera-*
tion in which shrapnel was removed and metal plate
inserted.

114. **X-RAY OF HEAD BEFORE OPERA-**
TION—Marion Greenwood.

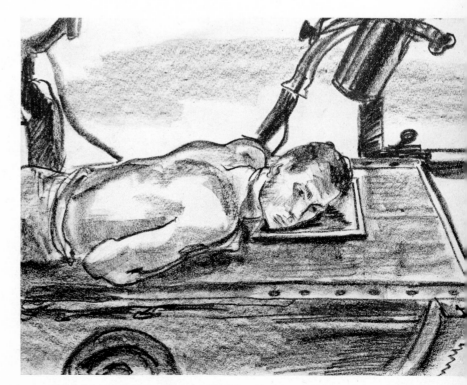

115. MEN WITH GOD—Robert Benney. *A few minutes before this badly wounded Pacific campaigner succumbed to the sting of a merciful needle he asked for the chaplain to come and pray with him. From American battle fronts all over the world comes the ringing message that there are no atheists in foxholes. To that message this canvas writes a resounding "Amen." Two men of God—and a Book.*

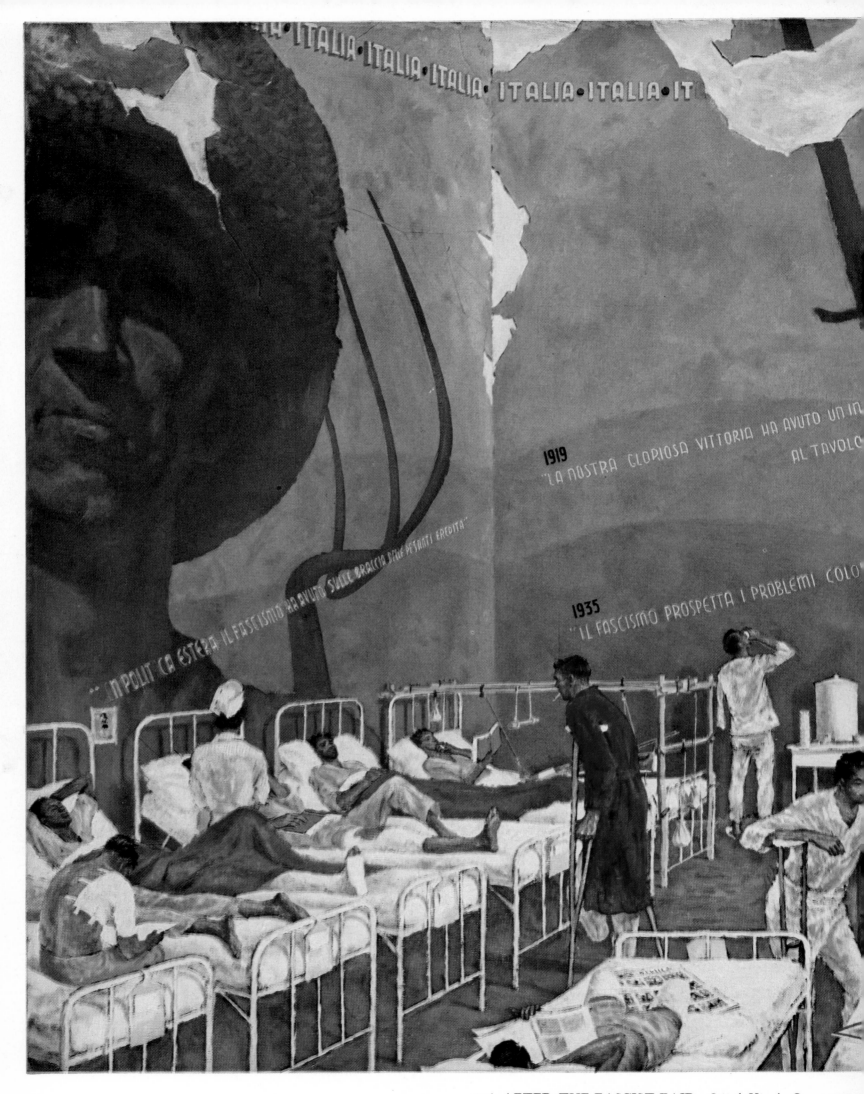

116. **AFTER THE FASCIST FAIR**—Joseph Hirsch. *Once upon a time Il Duce held a Fascist festival in a great, white building in Naples. People from miles around came to the city to view the ambitious murals and read the windy phrases of the bombastic Mussolini. But that was before Cassino and Anzio—before American doughboys climbed up the Italian*

boot and chased the flatulent dictator toward Berlin. Now Mussolini's
propaganda palace is an evacuation hospital and the heroic figures on the
crumbling walls compete in vain with American pin-up girls for adoration
from GI Joe.

117. **TREATING A MULE**—Joseph Hirsch. *In this war of mechanized divisions and "dismounted" cavalry, the chief function of the Veterinary Corps is the inspection of meat for our troops. But Artist Hirsch found this traditional Army mule in Italy getting a dose of mineral oil. Pack mules frequently need a laxative when they return from combat areas. A rubber tube is inserted in the animal's nose, pushed down his gullet and the oil pumped through. The mule doesn't like it.*

118. **SO WHAT**—Joseph Hirsch. *Kipling said: "It was crawlin' and it stunk"—this thirsty medic says. "So what!"*

119. FIELD EXAMINATION—Joseph Hirsch. *Medical Corpsmen make a hasty examination of a soldier's leg wound before carrying him to a Battalion Aid Station. The wound is a painful one as the tense expression of the man indicates. A little "dope" will calm him down for the trip back to the doctors.*

120. **NIGHT SHIFT**—Joseph Hirsch. *Hidden from snipers' bullets by the darkness of an Italian night, the medics bring in wounded infantryman. Although they are carrying their burden down a rocky, slippery slope, the corpsmen keep the litter level at all times to make the journey easier for the wounded man. The rifle makes an excellent emergency splint for a shot-up leg—an old battlefield trick of the litter bearers. Carrying a loaded litter over terrain too rugged even for pack mules, taxes to the utmost the skill and endurance of the corpsmen.*

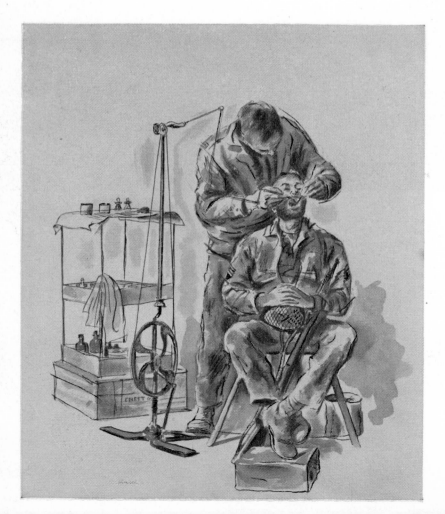

121. **FRONT-LINE DENTIST**—Joseph Hirsch. *The only kind of drilling they do at the front—sometimes within range of the enemy's howitzers.*

122. **SAFE**—Joseph Hirsch. *These little orphans know well that the Medical Corpsmen are the real liberators from pain and hunger.*

123. **PARADISE NOT LOST**—Joseph Hirsch. *Although he lost an arm in battle, this French Ghoum from North Africa is probably pleased that he did not suffer a head injury which would have resulted in the clipping of his queue to facilitate treatment. At death, the hand of Allah will grasp the precious queue and lift him to heaven.*

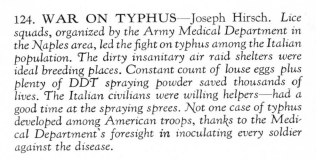

124. **WAR ON TYPHUS**—Joseph Hirsch. *Lice squads, organized by the Army Medical Department in the Naples area, led the fight on typhus among the Italian population. The dirty insanitary air raid shelters were ideal breeding places. Constant count of louse eggs plus plenty of DDT spraying powder saved thousands of lives. The Italian civilians were willing helpers—had a good time at the spraying sprees. Not one case of typhus developed among American troops, thanks to the Medical Department's foresight in inoculating every soldier against the disease.*

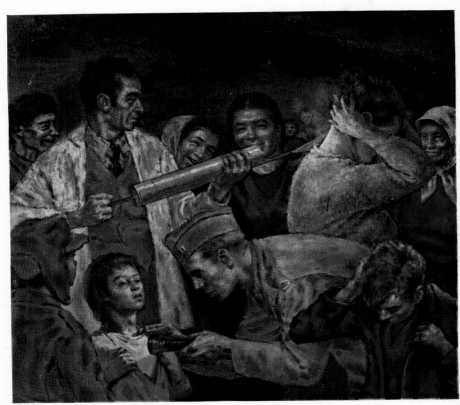

125. **ITALIAN RUSH HOUR**—Joseph Hirsch. *In this gay* u*
colored cartoon Artist Hirsch shows how an Army Field Hospital loo*
it passes through the main street of an Italian village en route to the Ca

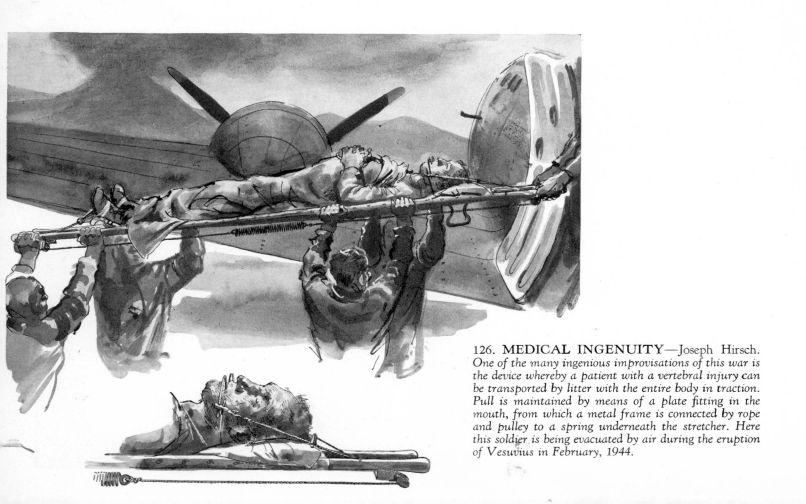

126. **MEDICAL INGENUITY**—Joseph Hirsch.
*One of the many ingenious improvisations of this war is
the device whereby a patient with a vertebral injury can
be transported by litter with the entire body in traction.
Pull is maintained by means of a plate fitting in the
mouth, from which a metal frame is connected by rope
and pulley to a spring underneath the stretcher. Here
this soldier is being evacuated by air during the eruption
of Vesuvius in February, 1944.*

Careful inspection of the picture will unearth many interesting side [...]
, such as the little boy waving a greeting with the American flag and
[co]lored soldier with a hot platter under his arm.

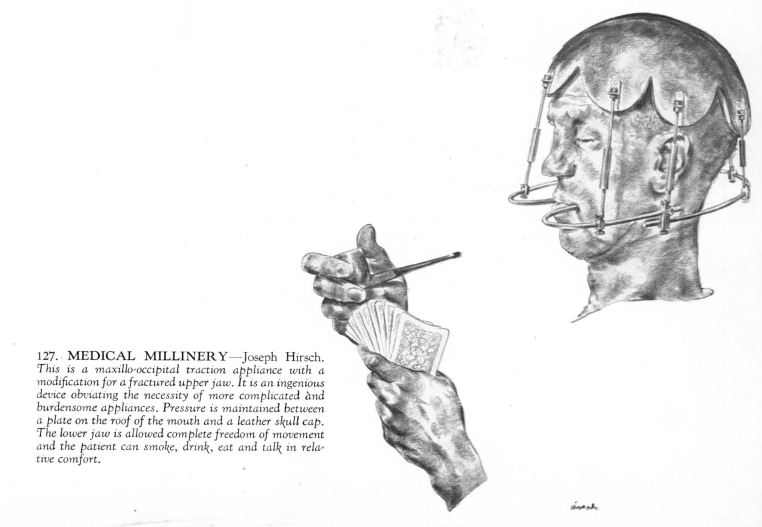

127. MEDICAL MILLINERY—Joseph Hirsch.
*This is a maxillo-occipital traction appliance with a
modification for a fractured upper jaw. It is an ingenious
device obviating the necessity of more complicated and
burdensome appliances. Pressure is maintained between
a plate on the roof of the mouth and a leather skull cap.
The lower jaw is allowed complete freedom of movement
and the patient can smoke, drink, eat and talk in rela-
tive comfort.*

128. **COMPANY IN THE PARLOR**—Joseph Hirsch. *The gaunt stone walls of an Italian farmhouse provide scant shelter for a front-line Battalion Aid Station, but they do screen the activities of the missing farmer's uninvited guests from the sharp eyes of enemy artillery spotters. Still under fire, the medics perform their duties with complete disregard for their own safety. Their only precaution seems to be to have the man at the left keep his binoculars trained on enemy guns and their targets of the moment. The parlor wall shrine makes an excellent medicine cabinet for drugs and antiseptics.*

129. ALL ABOARD FOR HOME—Joseph Hirsch. *One of the Army Medical Department's big hospital ships takes on wounded men during typical rainy day in England. When the ship arrives in New York, the men will be taken in ambulances to an East Coast Debarkation Hospital, from where many of them will be sent by hospital train to interior general hospitals for specialized treatment. Umbrellas are taboo in the Army, but Artist Hirsch insists his painting is authentic to the minutest detail.*

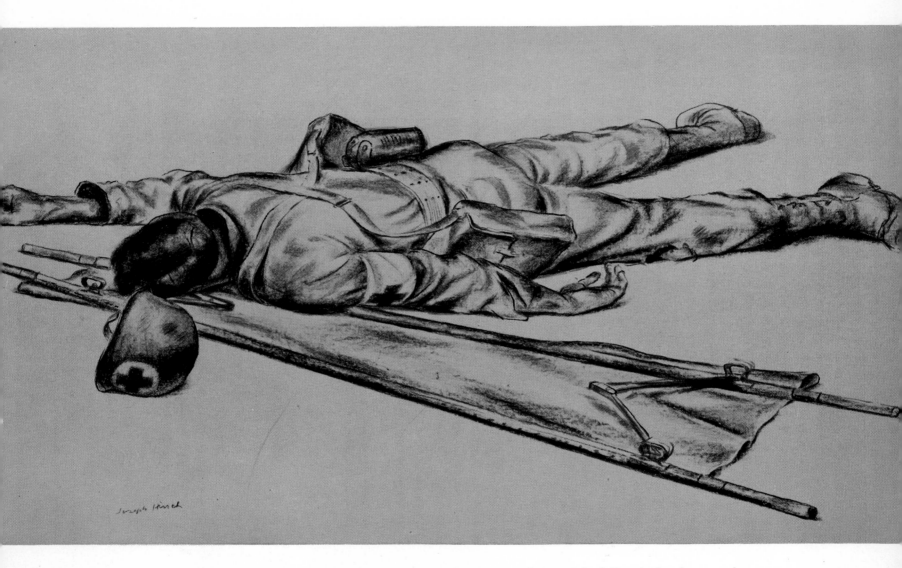

130. **NON-COMBATANT**—Joseph Hirsch. *Artist Hirsch found this Medical Corps enlisted man and his litter on an Italian front.*

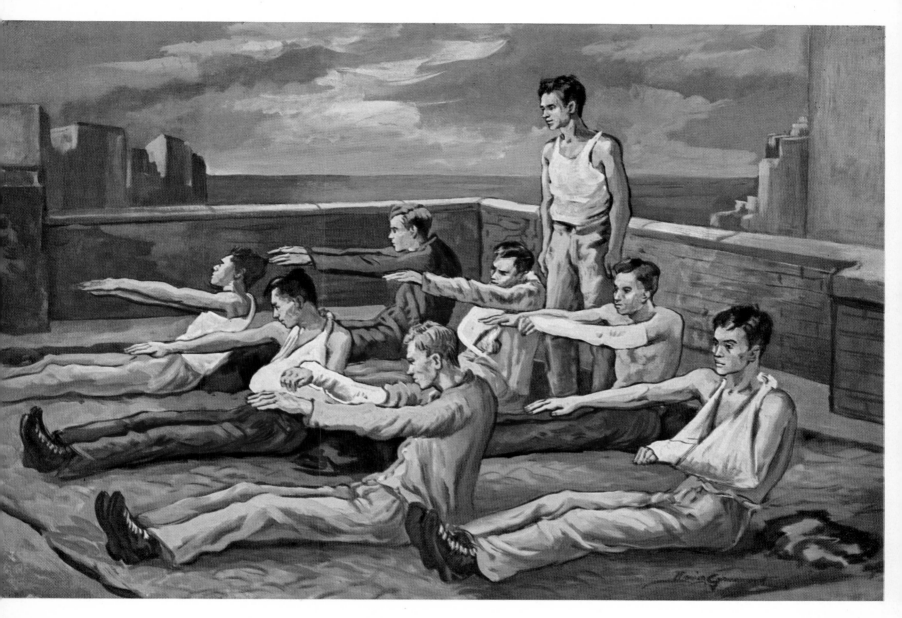

131. EXERCISE PERIOD FOR WOUNDED—Marion Greenwood. *These wounded men are determined, and their indomitable spirit is captured completely by Miss Greenwood's understanding brush. Despite the handicap of painful wounds encased in heavy, clumsy casts they struggle courageously to carry out the exercise routine prescribed for them. The Army Medical Department does not believe in inactivity during hospitalization —knows that men who exercise regularly recover quicker.*

132. **SHOULDER WHEEL**—Marion Greenwood.
Advanced Reconditioning following arm and shoulder injuries.

133. **STANDING-UP EXERCISES**—
Marion Greenwood. *Advanced Reconditioning. Homemade, simple devices made by veterans have proven best. Rollers are used for correcting ankle injuries.*

134. **A TWIST OF THE WRIST**—
Marion Greenwood. *Advanced Reconditioning. Apparatus for wrist exercises.*

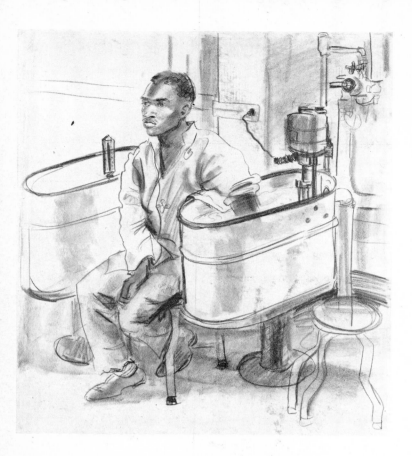

135. WHIRLPOOL BATH—Marion Greenwood.
Treatment for radial paralysis of left forearm.

136. GI GUTENBERG—Marion Greenwood. *Occupational therapy—Printing Press exercise for limbs and arms.*

137. FINGER EXERCISE—Marion Greenwood.
Modification of a Knaval Table.

The End

Illustrated with 118 plates in color

MEN WITHOUT GUNS
By DeWitt Mackenzie

WITH AN INTRODUCTION BY MAJOR GENERAL

NORMAN T. KIRK

SURGEON GENERAL OF THE UNITED STATES ARMY

THIS book records the great work of the Army Medical Corps in the war. In words and pictures the story is told of the services of our doctors, nurses, and enlisted men on the battlefields and in the hospitals of Europe and Asia. Packed with the dramatic tenseness and excitement of modern warfare, it is an authentic account of the men who fought without guns to save human life rather than destroy it.

DeWitt Mackenzie, of the Associated Press, whose graphic recital of the story behind the pictures reproduced in this book will hold the reader's attention from beginning to end, was a war correspondent in World War I, and as Associated Press war analyst during World War II covered the African, European, Burma, China, and Pacific fronts, where he saw the Army Medical Corps in action. From his firsthand knowledge of the various combat areas visited by the artists whose work is represented here, and from years of experience in gathering and presenting facts, he has succeeded in producing a contemporary record of extraordinary interest and permanent value.

A dozen American artists braved the hardships and perils of war to make the notable series of historical paintings, now the property of the United States Government, reproduced in MEN WITHOUT GUNS.